TAKING THE LEAP

From Employee or Executive to Female Founder

MARCIA BENCH
WITH 13 INSPIRING WOMEN

TAKING THE LEAP

MARCIA BENCH WITH 13 INSPIRING WOMEN

Copyright© 2024 Marcia Bench and High Flight Press - First Edition.

No part of this book may be reproduced or transmitted in any form or by any means, electronic or mechanical, including photocopying, recording or by any information storage and retrieval system, without written permission from the author, except for the inclusion of brief quotations in a review.

Disclaimer

This book is designed to provide information and motivation to our readers. It is sold with the understanding that the publisher is not engaged to render any type of psychological, legal, or any other kind of professional advice. The content of each article is the sole expression and opinion of its author, and not necessarily that of the publisher. No warranties or guarantees are expressed or implied by the publisher's choice to include any of the content in this volume. Neither the publisher nor the individual author(s) shall be liable for any physical, psychological, emotional, financial, or commercial damages, including, but not limited to, special, incidental, consequential or other damages. Our views and rights are the same: You are responsible for your own choices, actions, and results.

Permission should be addressed in writing to Marcia Bench or High Flight Press at **info@femalefoundersgrowthacademy.com**

Cover Design: Edith Wolek - edithwolek.com; edith@emperorsmedia.com

Book Design: Edith Wolek - edithwolek.com; edith@emperorsmedia.com

Dedicated to:

All the women who are yet
to step fully into their power and courage
to follow their vision and create
their own phenomenal results.

TABLE OF CONTENTS

INTRODUCTION *1*

CHAPTER 1
IT ALL COMES DOWN TO PURPOSE - MARCIA BENCH *5*

CHAPTER 2
CREATIVITY SAVED MY LIFE - BRANDI AHNER *19*

CHAPTER 3
NAVIGATING THE JOURNEY TO ENTREPRENEURSHIP: REFLECTION, RESILIENCE, REINVENTION - KIM E. ANDREWS. *31*

CHAPTER 4
NEVER STOP DREAMING - NICOLE ASPENSON *43*

CHAPTER 5
FROM SURVIVAL TO REVIVAL: TRANSFORMING LIFE ON YOUR OWN TERMS - TERRI BEARDSLEY *55*

CHAPTER 6
TRANSITION FROM CORPORATE MANAGER TO CAREER COACH: MY MIDLIFE LEAP - CAROL DAVIES *67*

CHAPTER 7
DR. MINDY'S 7 SECRETS: LIVING AN ADAPTIVE WORKLIFE - DR. MINDY GEWIRTZ *79*

CHAPTER 8
STEPPING INTO THE POSSIBLE - LIZ HATCHER. *95*

CHAPTER 9
THE CIRCUS, DEFINING NORMAL, AND CHOOSING YES! - ALLISON KEELEY *105*

CHAPTER 10
THE DIARY OF A DIVA: UNBREAKABLE SPIRIT - DAWN RENEE . . . *117*

CHAPTER 11
LESSONS FROM THE BRINK OF DEATH - RUKSHANA TRIEM *127*

CHAPTER 12
FROM SHADOWS TO SPOTLIGHT: EMBRACING PASSION TO TRANSFORM LIVES - EDITH WOLEK. *139*

CHAPTER 13
FROM ENABLER, TO ENLISTED, TO ENTREPRENEUR - APRIL YOUNG. *151*

CHAPTER 14
THE $300 GAMBLE: FROM CORPORATE BURNOUT TO BUILDING A SUCCESSFUL BUSINESS - JAMIE YOUNG *167*

INTRODUCTION

If you are reading this book, chances are you are either in a corporate role now and wanting to take charge of your future by starting your own business, or you are already a female founder and looking for inspiration from other women like you.

The good news is that for years now, women have been starting businesses at twice the rate of men. But the other news is that they tend not to hire help as quickly, and they earn less than male founders. A full 90 percent of female-owned businesses will never reach six figures.

And let's face it - the environment around us is volatile. There are economic ups and downs and political unrest, coupled with the unexpected detours life hands us in our personal and family life. So with the relative ease of starting a side hustle online today, it makes sense that every female corporate executive should at least have a side hustle, whether they intend to go full-time with it in the future or not.

That is how nearly every one of our authors started out, including me. In my case, it became impossible to ignore the calling of my creative self as I started my career as a lawyer. And while the facts and circumstances of the stories you were about to read are different, not one of them regrets taking the leap to being a female founder.

In fact, it turns out that entrepreneurship is the most rigorous personal and spiritual growth path one will ever embark upon. Learning to be vulnerable and sharing our stories, as each of these women here have done, takes courage. Learning to not only perfect the craft required for our offerings, but also to create the infrastructure required in running a business, is an ongoing educational process. And the challenges change at every level of growth.

It is my hope, as the compiler of these amazing stories, that you will find yourself in at least one of them. If you have not yet taken the leap to start your own business - even part-time - I believe you will be inspired to do so. And if you have, you will recognize some of the challenges the co-authors have overcome, as well as the victories they have achieved.

One of the things that can make being a female founder challenging is not being understood by others. Family, friends, and others we know who work within the traditional 9 to 5 job model are wired differently than entrepreneurs. That results in some female employees and executives staying longer than they should in their corporate job due to fear of losing the perceived security that they have there. But all it takes is one unexpected layoff, or that meeting where you are discounted or taken for granted once again, for you to realize there must be more to life and work than this.

Like anything in life, starting and growing your own business has new challenges around every corner. But the rewards of being able to create your own map for the future, to work when, where, and with whom you want, to enjoy work and life harmony, and to remove the upper limits on your income are well worth it.

As you read this book, you'll laugh, you'll cry, and you'll be inspired to step into your next level self. We invite you to reach out to those authors with whom you particularly relate and let them know how much you appreciated their sharing their story. And if you are ready to take that leap yourself, join our online community and reach out for support. It's there waiting for you.

To your ongoing success,

Marcia Bench

CHAPTER 1

Marcia Bench

IT ALL COMES DOWN TO PURPOSE

My initial leap into entrepreneurship came with a jolt. I was awakened from a deep sleep one Saturday night, and instantly the concept and content for my first book began to download. I turned on the light and began writing what I was receiving. I knew not only what book I needed to write and what to include, but also the class that I wanted to teach and where to pitch it. This inspiration gave me a side hustle (although we didn't call it that back then) that ended up opening the door to many exciting opportunities. By that time, I had completed college and obtained my psychology degree. I had also graduated from law school and passed the Bar exam. But I wasn't convinced that being a lawyer was the right path for me. There was no place for my creative self to express in the legal field.

I was born with not only intellectual prowess, but a strong dose of creativity. I started piano lessons at the age of eight when my parents noticed my desire to learn. Growing up as the child of a farmer and a secretary, money was tight. But somehow, they came up with the money to buy a piano from my dad's boss at his part-time job. I studied piano for 12 years and minored in music in college.

My brother and I even put on little stage shows in our basement for the family around the Christmas season, making our own backdrop, and writing the whole thing. I loved writing from the time I could pick up a pen.

But creative writing was one thing - writing legal briefs was another. It was a completely different style, and I was dedicated to learning it so I could be successful in that profession.

Nevertheless, my creative self would not be quelled. I followed the guidance I got that Saturday night, approached the local community college's continuing education department about teaching a class on consumer rights, and they approved my request.

I wrote the book and taught the class.

(Surprisingly, the readership for that self-published spiral bound book turned out not to be primarily consumers but attorneys. Since the primary lawyers' guidebook on that area of the law was not being kept up to date, my treatment of the subject was a welcomed resource.)

I continued my relationship with that continuing education department, teaching one one-day class per quarter. It was the perfect opportunity to try out new topics, many related to entrepreneurship, as I began to work more with business owners in my law practice - including women wanting to start a business.

Meanwhile, I was on my own quest to clarify my life purpose. At age 14, I started asking my minister, my parents, my teachers, and others how to find my purpose. I went to classes. I read books. But as the saying goes, the answer to my quest was hidden in the place where it was least likely to be found: within the recesses of my own mind and soul.

The day I filed my papers with the state making my side hustle an official business, my purpose suddenly became clear. I had lost interest in every job that I had had in the past - usually after just a few months. It felt like "been there, done that - what's next?"

But intuitively, I knew that as an entrepreneur there would be enough roles to assume and tasks to complete that it would keep me occupied for a lifetime. And it has!

I realized that, after my 18 years of study, introspection, and seeking answers from outside sources, I had to share what finally worked for me in discovering my life purpose. So I went to the community college continuing ed department again with a new idea: I wanted to teach a course called Increasing Fun and Satisfaction at Work. It would help the college students and professionals who attended the professional development classes discover meaning and purpose in their work - whether that was what they were currently doing or something new.

What happened next was nothing short of remarkable: when we listed the class on the next quarter's schedule, it was completely full three weeks before it was scheduled to be presented. That had never happened before, so I knew I was onto something. I taught that class sharing quotes (with credit, of course!) from books such as *Do What You Love and the Money Will Follow*, *Work with Passion*, and the like, leading the group through exercises drawn from the books.

It was a rousing success, and many of the participants had huge breakthroughs. As I continued working with this idea, I was able to develop 10 clues to discovering your life purpose that I continue to share to this day. I shared them in an article for *Science of Mind* magazine, and it was one of the most widely read articles I ever wrote.

I was still practicing law by day, teaching one Saturday per quarter at the college, and consulting with a few private clients. I begin offering consulting packages on the topic of discovering your life purpose and incorporating it into your work.

Meanwhile, work at the law firm was becoming untenable. One dispute over a business sale gone bad ended up occupying the entire workload of two of the partners and me. I learned a key lesson about myself then: I not only liked variety in my work - I required it. And I no longer had it, having to face this case every single day.

I sent out dozens of resumes, seeking work with another law firm. I got no interviews. I dropped a dozen or so copies off with the Oregon Bar Association, since they sometimes knew of open positions. But day after day, the drudgery went on.

I learned about the practice of visioning and decided to try it. I took out a yellow legal pad and hand wrote my vision of what I called an ideal "work opportunity" - for some reason I didn't call it a job - including the ideal hours, duties, setting, and lifestyle that I desired to have. I did this every night before bed for weeks.

One day I got a call from a gentleman, identifying himself and the company he worked for, and saying that he wanted to chat with me. I turned him down. I didn't want to work for the kind of company he represented.

But he didn't give up. He called again a couple weeks later, and I turned him down again. But as the drudgery continued, and no other opportunities were emerging, I finally said yes when he called the third time.

"I'll give you 15 minutes - no more," I said.

So we met for coffee. Apparently, he had picked up my résumé from the Oregon State Bar Association where I had left those copies weeks ago.

When he began to share the details of what he was looking for, my jaw dropped. His company was looking for in-house counsel on a part-time basis. They would provide an office, a secretary, and all of the office equipment that I would need. I just needed to dedicate 10 to 20 hours a week to them, signing required documents and appearing in court on occasion. The rest of the time I was free to serve my own legal clients and to do whatever else I might wish to do - which, at that time for me, was expanding my consulting practice.

I recognized this opportunity was exactly what I was visioning in my daily writing exercise. But I nearly turned it away because of the kind of company this man represented: a collection agency. It's what Napoleon Hill means in his book *Think and Grow Rich*: "Opportunity often comes disguised in the form of misfortune or temporary defeat."

But he and the manager of the agency were very nice men - and the working conditions were very appealing - so I took the job. The retainer was very small, but I had a base from which to launch more consulting as well as take on my own clients, so I was thrilled. I signed about 70 garnishments (with multiple carbon copies) daily, went to court maybe once a month for the occasional case that wouldn't settle, and it was great.

I even expanded into the neighboring office space when it became available and hired an associate. But I realized that as the business was growing, I needed additional marketing skills. I hired my very first mentor, and we began working together one on one. I also attended all of the live seminars she hosted, since she was local to my area in Portland, Oregon.

Like so many entrepreneurs, I struggled to niche down. And niching was her specialty.

One day I happened to have a book in my office that I had been inspired by. She picked it up and noticed it was published by Hay House, but it wasn't written by Louise Hay. As far as I knew up to that point, only books written by Louise herself were published by her publishing company. By this time, I had developed a proven system which helped people choose their career based around their life purpose and incorporate that purpose on a daily basis.

My mentor put two and two together and suggested that I approach Hay House about publishing the book I was beginning to conceptualize, to see if they would publish it. I did just that, submitting my proposal. I heard back from Reid Tracy (now president of the company, at that time on the editorial staff). We had a conversation, and they said yes. I became the third author they published after the gentleman whose book inspired me to reach out to them.

One of the areas of my business that I wanted to develop was professional speaking. I continued to present workshops at the community college. Occasionally a client would hire me to do training on employment law for their employees or managers, since that was one of the areas of law I specialized in. But I was struggling to find speaking gigs on larger stages where I could share my message.

One weekend, my husband and I decided to go to the beach, which was about an hour from where we lived. I found myself watching Tony Robbins' infomercial, Personal Power - which was running 24/7 on television.

He posed this power question: "What if you could start fulfilling your dream right now, and you didn't have to wait? What would be your first step?"

It hit me like a ton of bricks. I realized I not only knew the first step I would take - but the first three steps. And a plan was born.

I decided it was time to go all in on my work around life purpose and career. I offered to sell my law practice to my associate, and he accepted. I began writing my book, dedicating one hour every morning, before I drove downtown to my office, to the writing process. We put our house on the market, and it sold. We bought an RV to live in and begin outfitting it with our needed supplies for a year-long seminar tour around the United States.

I contacted an influencer who was well-respected among a chain of nonprofit organizations. She wrote a reference letter for me. I sent that letter out to all of the various outlets and began booking stops on my tour. I even put together a dummy version of what would become *When 9 to 5 Isn't Enough* (the Hay House book), to sell along the way.

Six months after that day at the beach, my national book/seminar tour began. (As you might expect, Hay House wasn't exactly thrilled that I was selling the book ahead of their publication date, but they just simply accelerated the release to tap into the publicity and sales opportunities of my tour.)

I only had nine stops booked when I left on the tour, but I had faith that the rest of the calendar would fill in. By the time I returned to Oregon ten months later, I had presented 65 seminars. I call it my "Toastmasters in the trenches." It was a challenging way to learn speaking skills - and trust me, the first workshop was far less polished than the last! I learned to require a minimum fee, since some of the audiences were small. And I became well known within the sphere of those nonprofits.

While I was doing a book signing at a downtown Portland bookstore, I discovered that I was on the front page of the Living section of the *Oregonian* newspaper with my story. That same day, the local ABC affiliate called me to do an appearance. Everything converged, like the cherry on a sundae.

After the national tour, I wasn't sure what to do next, so I ultimately ended up going to work for a seminar company. I was thrilled to have been chosen out of 200 applicants - but that excitement didn't last long. The owners of this locally based company were penny pinchers. They would send each of us presenters out on a two-day run, where we hosted two three-hour seminars the first day, then drove to a new city and did two more, returning home that night. It was exhausting.

I remember one stop in Canada during the winter where they nonchalantly plopped a battery charger in my back seat.

"You'll need this in the snowy sub-zero weather we're expecting," they said.

I didn't "do" snow. And I think that was the last straw. I was done.

So, it turned out, was my health. I had a massive health crisis and was unable to work for the following year due to consequences of alcohol abuse, adrenal exhaustion and chronic fatigue. I had to reclaim myself, living on borrowed funds and the kindness of strangers. And ultimately, my marriage didn't survive.

It was at that time that I met my current husband of 30 years - on the driveway of a mutual friend. I had just left my previous marriage that day - so I felt anything but ready for a new relationship. But he knew instantly.

We began dating and were married two years later. I had returned to consulting on my own, and then took a position with a career consulting firm for a year.

My husband decided to retire two years early - and we wanted to find a warmer place to live than Portland. So we bought an RV, sold our home (sound familiar?) and traveled that year, exploring the desert southwest and the southeastern U.S.

We decided to choose the location where we would land based on where I got a job or business opportunity, rather than deciding randomly. And since I'd been doing a bit of consulting for that same firm while on the road, they asked me to help start and staff their new San Diego office. I said yes - so we parked the RV on the waterfront in San Diego, and I showed up for my first day of work.

Imagine my surprise when I saw nothing but boxes everywhere - no desks. I had consulting candidates to interview and had to sit on an upside-down box to do the interview. (My professional self was quite embarrassed!)

Soon we bought a home in San Diego and sold the RV. And even though I was working in an employed position, I intuitively knew I would be an entrepreneur again in the future. So I kept my supplies from my previous entrepreneurial ventures until the time was right.

Working at that company was dysfunctional from the start - and it worsened as this family-owned business decided to try to go public during the dot-com boom. I couldn't stand the unethical practices - and I wanted out. I didn't want to be associated with that type of company. But

I lasted five years, coaching 100 clients per year (including full days in person) and managing a staff of five. I coped by drinking more and more - whether I was in town or in the other state where I was flown every other week to do consulting at the home office. I was miserable.

One day, when my assistant delivered the mail, there was a flyer addressed to me about something called coaching, which I hadn't heard of until then (outside of the sports industry). I couldn't attend the program that was being advertised, but I wanted to learn more.

I arranged to have breakfast with the Program Director of the sponsoring organization on a Friday morning - when I got back from my next out-of-town trip. She told me more about what coaching was and said that she had enrolled in a coach training program scheduled to begin the following Monday. She also said there was one additional spot available in the training. If I was interested, she suggested I contact the training provider and see if I could still get in. I spent the weekend doing my due diligence and talking with the head of the training company. I took a big, deep breath, gave him my credit card number, and jumped in.

By this time, I had already written and published several books - both self-published and with Simon & Schuster, was consulting 100 clients per year, and saw myself as fairly well skilled and well educated in the professional services arena. I knew that I would pick up some additional strategies, tools, and tips from the coach training. But I had no idea that I would feel like Alice entering Wonderland when I attended that first teleclass the following Monday.

The other members of the class were also well educated and there to advance their learning. I discovered that coaching was completely different from consulting, and I was delighted at the prospect of being in the moment, asking coaching questions, and not having to have the answers all of the time.

I completed that first six-month certification, attending the classes from home when I was in San Diego, and from my hotel during the weeks that I was out of town. I continued on to get my master level certification with that training company as well. This was before easy access to web conferencing such as Zoom for everyday people. I wanted to learn how to speak without a live audience, so I enrolled in a training to become a teleclass leader.

When Thanksgiving came, my husband and I decided to spend it with my parents, who had retired to the Phoenix, Arizona area. I knew that when I got back from the holiday weekend, I was going to have to present a teleclass which was required to complete my teleleader certification. I hadn't yet decided what my topic would be.

Driving across the desert at dusk, with the top down in our convertible, I had another lightning-bolt moment. I suddenly realized that I could blend the coaching I had just learned with my years of career development experience and use that for my topic.

And even more than that, I could turn it into an online school - the first ever to teach career coaching. I was jazzed!!

Two months later, Career Coach Institute launched. Its base was the front one-third of our guest room in the San Diego house - using the supplies I had kept for the right time. And what we taught our coaches was those very same 10 clues to your life purpose that I had identified in my early days as a consultant.

This was 2001, and the coaching industry was only a few years old. There were only a few dozen coaching schools (compared to hundreds now). With the help of the Director of the coaching school I had attended, I was able to create a simple website for my training company. I began doing introductory teleclasses every other week to invite people into the certification. And when the first student wanted to enroll, I didn't even have a payment portal through which she could pay! I quickly got that in place and processed her tuition.

I ran that company for 19 years, overcoming breast cancer and resulting treatments in year two of the business. My team and I expanded it into 42 countries and I spoke at many international conferences - on those larger stages that I longed for in my days as a lawyer. We served thousands of students, and I was able to present staff training to multiple workforce development centers and college admissions staff as well.

Unlike many coaching schools, we also taught marketing and business building skills to our students. It was definitely a crowning achievement. But after all those years, I became restless again. I met with a business broker and covertly made it known that the company was for sale. I went through three painful experiences with prospective buyers. One was prepared to pay us a significant sum, and the deal was to close while my husband and I were in Nassau, Bahamas on vacation. I kept walking from one end of the hotel to the other - from our room to the business center where the fax machine was - awaiting news of the signed contract. But it never came. The recession had begun, enrollments were soft, and he withdrew his offer.

Regardless, I continued to explore opportunities and eventually did sell the company on March 3, 2020. I already knew what I was going to do next, so as soon as the funds cleared my bank, I hired a mentor. On March 10, the COVID-19 lockdown happened. I was so grateful that I was already doing online coaching and training (unlike many businesses who had to quickly pivot to online offerings) - so I doubled down on offering business building services for spiritually minded entrepreneurs. We closed millions of dollars in coaching during the three years of the Pandemic.

I have continued my writing, speaking and coaching. This book is number 30 in my portfolio. I am honored to be able to co-create it with 13 other amazingly capable women whom I have met along the way. I continue to navigate the ebbs and flows of the online marketplace, learning and relearning strategies that are effective now. I currently serve as founder and CEO of Female Founders Growth Academy (founded in 2024), which helps female founders create rapid growth using authority-building organic marketing strategies.

I know that the insights I had about my purpose when I incorporated my very first company turned out to be true. I am here to help other women entrepreneurs and female founders discover their life's purpose and use it to create a thriving business and massive impact. I will continue doing so until my days on the planet are complete.

ABOUT MARCIA BENCH

Marcia Bench

Marcia Bench is an Online Marketing Strategist for Female Founders. As the CEO of Female Founders Growth Academy, she helps women entrepreneurs apply proven online marketing strategies to grow their business and their thought leadership. In 2001, Marcia established the first career coach training school in the world, grew it to span 42 countries.

Marcia was the third author published by Hay House, and in addition to her 24 self-published books, she has been published by Simon & Schuster, Hasmark and other publishing houses.

Her other 29 books include *The Coach's AI Marketing Handbook*, *The Tao of Entrepreneurship*, *Success by the Numbers*, *Career Coaching: An Insider's Guide*, and *The High-Ticket Group Coaching Method*.

She is a frequent presenter at conferences, trade associations, corporations and universities. A former attorney and corporate executive, she is based in the Portland, Oregon area.

Website: https://femalefoundersgrowthacademy.com
Facebook: https://www.facebook.com/marcia.bench
Facebook group: https://www.facebook.com/groups/growthforfemalefounders
LinkedIn: https://www.linkedin.com/in/marciabench/
Instagram: https://www.instagram.com/marciabenchmarketer/

CHAPTER 1

CHAPTER 2

Brandi Ahner

CREATIVITY SAVED MY LIFE

May 31, 2024, felt like my final day on earth. We had just attended a party where my boyfriend at the time continued to drink way past his limits. He stayed until 2 a.m. when everyone except the place's owners left. If I hadn't called a Lyft, he would never have left.

When we left, instead of reflecting on our fantastic night and the great people we had connected with, he decided to focus on something that hadn't even happened and start a fight over it. We left around 2 a.m.… that's the beginning of my life flipping upside down. My arms were crossed. He hit me across my left arm, also hitting my right hand - and I knew what he was capable of after that first blow, knowing his background and having spent two and a half years with him. His emotional and verbal abuse had been subtly increasing day by day. And he had just said he wanted to murder me.

It was 2 a.m., no one was around. I clenched the sheet of the hotel bed I was in - cold and wet from the glass of water he had flung across the room in the middle of his rage.

I was terrified and legitimately wondered if I was going to lose my life that night. My screams in the hotel room fell on deaf ears.

My blood was racing, my heart was pounding, and my mind was sorting out all my potential options.

I felt utterly defenseless. I thought to myself, "What am I going to do?

When he finally passed out, I seized my chance. Sneaking into the bathroom, I called the front desk and told them I needed help and to call the police, my heart pounding with fear and desperation. I told the police about his background:
- He's trained to fight in martial arts
- He's a former Ranger Battalion trained to kill
- He owns a very large number of weapons.
- He is also bipolar and diagnosed with IED (intermittent explosive disorder).

Knowing that the police called in three more squad cars for backup before even approaching him, for a total of eight cops to protect themselves from him.

I thought surely they would at least take him to jail.
But amazingly, after talking with him, they let him walk free and even told him where I was headed, which led to him following me. That's why I lost nearly everything I owned.

How does it make sense that several grown men needed protection from this dangerous guy, yet they served me up on a silver platter and left me alone to fend for myself? He would surely be even more dangerous to me after calling the cops on him. I was utterly flabbergasted. And that added to the trauma of the situation.

As I raced through the airport, my mind was racing to figure out how to get "home" before him.

We were scheduled to fly home together on American Airlines June 2nd. But I wasn't waiting till then. He would have seen me switch that flight as it was on his account. So, I went to the airline directly and got the first flight out. That ticket cost me $1,000. I was in panic mode, not knowing if I would see him at the airport. I was crying in the middle of the airport, in shock that this was happening.

No one asked me if I was okay. I had to approach staff members to get help.

The airline staff were as helpful as possible; some went above and beyond once they heard my story. They let me board first and switched my seat to the last row so I could see if he got on. They even made a buddy bag filled with all kinds of snacks, fancy ones that aren't usually offered, with a note for me.

I didn't have a chance to thank them properly in my state. I hope they see this and know how much I truly appreciate their kindness in my time of need.

The note read:

"Brandi,
Today may be a storm, but the sun will come out soon! We are proud of you for having the courage to leave, and we just know the best is yet to come!! Some things to remember... Bad days don't last forever. You are stronger than you think. Small steps are also progress.

And you are amazing just the way you are! Keep your head up and stay strong <3

<3 Your Flight Crew (DL2412)"

He never got on that plane.

While I was relieved, it was short-lived. I had no idea where he was or when he would be heading home.

While waiting for the flight to take off, I checked the Delta App. I remembered I had his login information. I logged on, and lo and behold, he booked a flight with Delta, abandoning the American flight as I did. I had wished he had kept the flight for the next day, allowing me time to get my things.

He was on the flight immediately after me!

I couldn't believe it. I Could see where he was at, but the amount of time I'd have to gather belongings was slim. I'd have about an hour.

As luck would have it, my flight ended up being delayed.
And he landed early.

The thought raced in my mind.

"Why are things working out in his favor?! He's the one with the money, his name on everything, all the control?"
The hour-long window I thought I would have turned into 20 minutes.

I got a ride from the airport and hightailed it to the house, setting a timer on my phone so I knew when I had to leave.
I spent 20 minutes gathering everything I could to fit in one car from the house in an absolute frantic state.

There was no time to get a moving truck or time to load everything I owned.

The timer went off. My time was up.

Heartbroken but with no time to mourn my losses, I ran. Leaving the pets and keepsakes that are irreplaceable.

I got in the car and left the $700,000 house I thought would be my forever home.

As soon as I pulled out of the driveway, I saw some of my stuff on the road in my rearview mirror.

My heart sank. "No!"

The latch in the back wasn't shut properly in the chaos of trying to get out of there.

Looking ahead, knowing he could show up any minute, I quickly hit reverse. I wasn't leaving anything else behind.

I threw everything back in the car, shut the hatch, and sped off.

Only to realize it had happened again!

I stopped, threw it all in, and returned to the car.

The Universe must have thought there wasn't enough drama in this situation because this happened a third time.

My panic intensified because I expected to see his truck pull up as I stood on the road.

My heart was racing and breaking, extreme terror taking over. I had the same feelings you have when you watch a scary movie, or something scares the hell out of you.
The latch was being blocked. I moved what was in the way, threw my stuff in the back again, and sped off in full panic mode, knowing there was a chance he would see me.

His truck could have blocked me. There were deep ditches on either side of the road and no way out the other way.

I was so terrified.
I just drove with nowhere to go. We had just moved to Mississippi and didn't really know anyone yet. I lived in a state of heightened fear from 2:30 a.m. on May 31 until I arrived in Michigan on Monday, June 3rd. I'm calmer now but still recovering.

My mind started to analyze what had happened. I couldn't believe this was where I was when, 24 hours before, I had one of the best experiences in a long time. I met some incredible entrepreneurs. He spent the night drinking and trying to find ways to get people to help him with his business, which is fizzling out. He drank so much that he was being inappropriate with me in the lobby at the event while people were heading to the after-party. That's when a shift happened. I knew this was not the person I was meant to be with.

Looking back on my relationship with David, there were early signs that I chose to overlook, attributing his occasional outbursts to his intermittent explosive disorder (IED). He would reassure me that his frustration wasn't aimed at me, which often eased my concerns. However, as time went on, those outbursts intensified and began to target me directly, exploiting my vulnerabilities.

Despite recognizing the warning signs, I felt trapped in the moment, believing I could navigate the situation. However, looking back, it's clear that I was simultaneously planning my exit. I was saving money whenever I could and working to ensure my children's safety while living through the trauma. I moved to Mississippi with David while they stayed in Michigan, believing that this distance would protect them.

Feeling unable to confide in anyone about the reality of our situation, I stayed with him until it became too dangerous for me to remain, even though I wasn't financially prepared to leave. His financial abuse significantly impacted my ability to gain financial health, making it difficult to prepare for my escape. I was doing everything I could to protect my kids and figure out a way to get myself safe. Unfortunately, I ran out of time before I could prepare financially, and that culminated in the day he hit me. This timeline illustrates how insidiously abuse can escalate and underscores the importance of recognizing early signs and taking decisive action to protect oneself.

Before my life took a dramatic turn, I was deeply immersed in my work and passion projects. My days were filled with the aromas of gourmet dishes I created in the kitchen, and my nights often extended into the early hours, painting until my heart felt light. My entrepreneurial spirit was thriving, and I was on the brink of launching a major rebrand for my wellness program, Creative Spark. But behind the scenes, my personal life was unraveling.

The abusive relationship I endured became a suffocating darkness. The manipulation and verbal assaults eroded my self-esteem, and the physical abuse left me in a state of constant fear. Leaving that environment was not just about stepping out of a door but about breaking free from chains tightening around me for years. The decision to leave was the most terrifying and empowering moment of my life, as my life was flipped upside down from luxury to living in a borrowed camper, facing the stark reality of starting anew.

After escaping, I started over in almost every sense - emotionally, materially, and professionally. I had lost nearly everything, but my undying passion for creativity remained. I turned to my culinary and artistic skills as a form of therapy. Cooking became a way to regain control and structure in my life. Each dish I crafted was a small victory, a testament to my resilience. On the other hand, painting was a means to process the complex emotions that words could not capture. Through these creative acts, I began to rebuild my life, piece by piece. Additionally, my love for creating videos, particularly on platforms like TikTok, became a cherished outlet, allowing me to share my journey and connect with others through visual storytelling.

With a background spanning 17 years in the culinary arts and more than 25 years of creating art, I have always known the importance of creativity. However, it was during the aftermath of my escape from abuse that I experienced its therapeutic power again. As a certified health coach and an Art Therapy Practitioner, I turned to what I knew best: using creativity to heal. Each brush stroke, video, and recipe developed during this time were not just steps toward creating something new - they were steps toward reclaiming my life.

I started my business, Creative Spark, to combine my passions for wellness coaching and the arts, aiming to provide a holistic approach to personal transformation.

The desire to regain control of my life after escaping an emotionally toxic relationship fueled my journey into entrepreneurship back in 2018. It was about creating a path aligned with my creativity, healing, and empowerment values.

During my escape, one of the things that fell out was some of my blank art canvases. I didn't see they were damaged in the falls until days later. The corner of four canvases was scuffed up, and one had two holes in the front towards the top.

At first, I was so upset that they were ruined. I didn't have the funds to buy new ones and wanted to use those to sell my art in an attempt to rebuild.

It took me a moment to process, and then I let creativity win. I'm painting those canvases and incorporating the holes into the art. The story and meaning of the art on those canvases have more depth because of what they and I went through - scars from our trauma.

I gradually regained calmness and strength amidst ongoing recovery. Throughout this tumultuous period, my business has been a guiding light for both my personal and professional transformation. Our mission is clear and unwavering: to harness the profound power of creativity in navigating life's challenges and fostering resilience. This chapter not only recounts my experiences but also encourages you to explore how embracing creativity can deeply impact your own journey, particularly if you're an entrepreneur facing unique obstacles.

As I navigated the initial phases of my recovery, I found solace in the kitchen, video content, and the canvas. Cooking became more than just a way to nourish my body; it was a ritual that helped me regain control over my life. Each dish I prepared was a step towards reclaiming my independence and a testament to my resilience. Similarly, painting and art became mediums through which I could express emotions too complex to articulate in words.

These creative outlets were not just hobbies; they were vital tools in my journey towards healing. They taught me the importance of patience, the value of small victories, and the incredible strength required to create something from nothing - lessons that are quintessential for any entrepreneur.

Through Creative Spark, I aim to facilitate profound personal transformations using creativity as a therapeutic tool. It's about empowering individuals to heal and thrive.

One of the biggest challenges I faced was rebuilding my client base and reputation after leaving my abusive relationship. It tested my resilience and determination to redefine the mission of my business.

And I have to share that I almost gave up on writing this chapter. But I remembered what I often share with others: giving up on difficult things makes things easy in the moment - but harder later.

What I didn't see coming when I started this book project was experiencing a very traumatic event.

While I am not unfamiliar with traumatic events, usually, people take time to process and heal what happens to them and then write a book about it years later. This is happening in real-time, leaving me either the option of giving up and turning on Netflix or writing the damn chapter. And I very much wanted to give up and hide from the world.

But as you can see, I wrote it. And I did it to show you exactly why I do what I do.

Writing this chapter amidst my trauma is not only tremendously difficult, but it exemplifies my commitment to resilience and perseverance. It showcases my dedication to overcoming adversity, choosing the path of courage over comfort, and utilizing creativity as a healing force, where writing becomes a creative act of resilience.

All to teach you that you can harness your creativity and inner strength to navigate challenges, rebuild your life, and embrace transformation with courage and creativity.

I didn't survive all the trauma I've been through to curl up and hide. And I wasn't going to wait for things to get better because some of you out there need my message now, just as others out there need yours.

For us entrepreneurs, creativity is not just about innovation or business ideas, but problem-solving and resilience. In the world of business, challenges are inevitable. Whether it's a funding issue, a market downturn, or internal team conflicts, the ability to think creatively about solutions is invaluable.

Creative Spark was reborn from this very premise. Instead of just focusing on business coaching or art classes, I decided we would now integrate the concept of holistic wellness through creativity. This not only differentiates us in a competitive market, but also provides a more profound value to our clients: the tools to transform their own challenges into opportunities.

Throughout my journey as an entrepreneur, I've learned to embrace persistence, authenticity, and adaptability as the guiding principles that helped me overcome challenges in my business and personal life. These principles enabled me to pivot, innovate, and remain steadfast in pursuing my mission even during the toughest times. Collaborating with a mentor provided invaluable guidance and perspective along the way. Reflecting on my experiences of adversity and transformation, I've come to appreciate the profound impact of creativity in healing and empowering oneself.

As you navigate your entrepreneurial path, remember that creativity isn't just about innovation in business - it's also a powerful tool for personal growth and resilience. Embrace your creativity to solve business challenges, heal, and drive positive change in your life. I encourage you to tap into your unique creative spirit to find solutions and insights to propel you forward on your journey!

ABOUT BRANDI AHNER

Brandi Ahner

Introducing Brandi, founder of BranDiva Creative-Spark Wellness Studio and passionate advocate for using art as a tool for healing and personal transformation. With over a decade of personal development experience and a background as a professional chef and certified health coach, Brandi has dedicated her life to helping others unleash their creativity, and cultivate inner peace.

As a creative wellness advocate, Brandi believes in the power of artistic expression to facilitate healing and promote emotional well-being. Her artwork, intentionally crafted to resonate with the themes of healing and self-discovery, is also available for sale.

Through her workshops, Brandi guides individuals on a transformative journey of self-exploration and growth. Inspired by her own experiences of overcoming trauma and finding healing through art, she inspires others to embrace their unique gifts, unleash their creativity, and live authentically. Her coaching sessions are designed to empower individuals to take charge of their personal growth.

Web: https://www.artpal.com/brandiva22
Facebook: https://www.facebook.com/22BranDiva/
TikTok: https://www.tiktok.com/@brandiva22

Kim E. Andrews

NAVIGATING THE JOURNEY TO ENTREPRENEURSHIP: REFLECTION, RESILIENCE, REINVENTION

Sometimes, even when the signs are there, it's hard to hear your calling.

There was the time when I attended a mandatory senior leadership program. One of my personality assessments showed that the characteristics of the role I was in compared to what gave me joy and satisfaction were total opposites. The trainer of that program later whispered in my ear, "You must be extremely stressed. Take care of yourself."

There were the medical visits where my work was leading to declining breast health multiple times.

And even worse, after a period of working nights and weekends for months, I came home to find that the arrangement of my home had changed - even the organization of the refrigerator was different. Why?

The reason is that I wasn't home a lot, or when I was, I was just mentally exhausted, so my husband started naturally taking care of things. We didn't want to hire a cleaning person, and I intuitively felt there was more going on with me that needed to be resolved. I needed to find time to care for myself, spend more time at home, and just rest… but it didn't happen.

I eventually figured out that even though I was progressing in the organization I worked for, my spirit and soul were not - which in turn affected my physical and mental health. Upon that awareness, I put in a six-week notice (enough time to allow me to complete some major projects). During this time, I had no idea what I was going to do after I left the company… I just knew it was time for a new career path - and fast!

That was my turning point from corporate to entrepreneurship. This new journey would include starting my own business. But doing what… I had no freaking idea at that time! All I felt at the time was an internal desire to follow my heart. I rested, prayed, and walked a lot to clear my head. During this time, I didn't feel scared or have any doubts. It just felt right.

Perhaps being an entrepreneur was in my blood from the beginning. I entered this world prematurely in a small Kansas town. When I was just three months old, my family relocated to Denver, Colorado. Denver back then was not the bustling city it is today. It was a smaller city where I was raised in a middle-class African American neighborhood as the oldest of three siblings - a younger sister and brother. Our family environment was characterized by diligence, support, and entrepreneurship - all of which would shape my future.

From a young age, I was drawn to learning. Every summer, starting from sixth grade to my first year in college, I voluntarily attended summer school. It was my "thing;" I would walk, take the bus by myself, or get a ride from my parents - using any means available to have fun with friends and learn. It was a different time, one where independence and self-sufficiency were supported.

My grandfather on my father's side was entrepreneurial; he owned a small farm in Kansas where I was born. Every summer, we would visit the farm where we rode on tractors, fed hogs, petted horses, and saw cows being milked.

My father, on the other hand, was educated and diligent. He worked three jobs: a city job, a part-time accountant for the first black financial institution in Denver, and real estate sales. My mother was also college-educated, though she didn't have a formal degree. She worked for the city, was also a licensed Head Start teacher, and directed many of the programs.

There was never any question about us attending college in our household. My dad made it clear that college was part of the plan. He was so driven he wanted my sister and me to obtain a real estate license by the time we reached eighth grade. Obviously, that couldn't happen; we were too young, but his drive made an impact on me and set a foundation for my future ambitions.

My first non-paying job was helping out in the administration office of my middle school. That led to my first real paying job - working a few hours a day in a hospital pharmacy during the summer where I literally counted pills to place in pharmaceutical bottles. Can you imagine a 14-year-old counting pills today? Mind-blowing, right?

My goal to work was to buy a new "hot pants" outfit and a ticket to a local concert - which was a big deal then. I met the goal, wore the cute outfit, and had a great time at the concert with friends.

My college journey was far from smooth sailing. I struggled - and even flunked out of college my junior year. But I kept at it, working and attending various schools part-time to complete my degree. I attended a Jesuit college, a community college, and an HBCU (historically black college and university) - and still no degree, but plenty of debt. It felt like a huge burden.

During that time, my father sat me down to offer some sound and memorable advice that would shape my future approach to education and career choices. He encouraged me to stop school temporarily and gain real work experience, then return to school where my work knowledge would help me connect the dots between academics and real life. So I shifted my focus.

Following my dad's guidance, I spent the next five years working in the accounting departments of the banking and oil and gas industries. That was where I experienced my first and second layoffs. But it was the oil and gas company where I discovered my interest in working with both numbers and people. This landed me in the Personnel (now known as Human Resources) department for a short period before the final layoff.

Being laid off allowed me time to reflect on my career path and to decide what to do next, while I worked temporary jobs. Although I explored network marketing opportunities due to my entrepreneurial inclination, I quickly recognized that my strengths lay elsewhere.

Guided by career counselors at my church who shared the results of a few career assessments with me, it was clearly obvious that Human Resources (HR) would be a good fit for me. So, I pursued opportunities in HR within large corporations and popular banks, but those doors of opportunity weren't opening for me. That was a tough realization for me!

The biggest disappointment was being rejected by the Bell Company after failing their management assessment. It was a true turning point for me. I then realized the importance of working for a company whose values aligned with my values.

Within a month of that realization, a friend working at a quasi-government organization hired me into their internal clerical pool within HR. I quickly realized how that organization's values were very much aligned with mine. Within three months, I received a promotion to supervise that same clerical pool.

Over the years I worked there, I got promoted five times, eventually becoming Senior HR Officer. In that role, I supervised and managed benefits, compensation, recruitment, and employee relations, and also oversaw payroll and special projects.

And by the way, my father was right! While working full-time at this organization, I graduated with honors, obtaining a bachelor's degree from a private university where I attended full-time on weekends. Hard work, but I finally finished what I started!

Life took a significant turn after that last promotion. I got married and relocated to Nashville, Tennessee. I knew with so many changes happening all at once in my life - a new marriage, new city, no family or friends, no job - I needed a game plan to get acclimated to all the newness in my life.

I joined Mary Kay® as a beauty consultant to network with other women and follow my entrepreneurial tendency. Simultaneously, I worked temporary jobs to familiarize myself with various companies throughout the city. Nashville at the time was primarily known as a mid-size country music city, not the thriving major city it is now.

My first substantial professional role was at a prominent university in the area. I worked in their HR department, where I made compensation decisions and supported a multitude of employees across their university, medical school, medical clinic, and hospital. This position provided a wealth of learning opportunities. Although the work was great, the pay wasn't.

I then accepted an opportunity at a large national hospitality company in their HR department, where I met wonderful people, and celebrities and enjoyed the perks of concerts and country music. After a couple of years, my position moved to New York, and I had to job search for new opportunities fairly quickly. I landed a new position before the company completed the organizational restructure.

What lay ahead for me was totally unexpected on my life's journey, leading to stress, health concerns, and self-discovery. I took a position with a prominent Chicago insurance company within their HR department located in Nashville as an HR Consultant to employees in different geographical locations.

The role was challenging with few rewards, and the stress began to take a toll on my breast health. It took me three alarm clocks - I kid you not, three different alarms - to drag myself out of bed each morning.

Heeding my doctor's advice to find ways to alleviate stress before my health became more serious, I needed an exit plan. I saved up money to hold me for a short time, then submitted my resignation notice. My journey toward improved health, self-discovery, and entrepreneurship began. Within the time-period of putting in my notice, I slept better and only needed one alarm clock to get up. And lastly, the results of my "final" breast assessment eventually showed a clean bill of health shortly after leaving the company.

I decided to take time off to visit family and friends, worked temporary jobs again, and did some side recruiting work in hopes of opening my own business. But instead, I met a recruiter who connected me with an international manufacturing and distribution company.

The company was looking for an HR Manager to work temporarily for three months while their manager was on maternity leave, which eventually led to a regular full-time opportunity for me.

I started managing one employee, then overseeing employees nationally and internationally, and also became an active part of the senior management team, answering to the president and traveling internationally as a Senior Managing Director. It offered professional development, new challenges to overcome, work experiences, and overall personal growth and awareness.

But, I was extremely stressed. I refused to take work home, so I worked late, "a lot", including weekends. And just because I didn't physically take work home, I did mentally.

I was definitely considered a company woman, and after four years, the president hired an Executive Coach for me to better position me for a higher-level role. However, the familiar pattern of stress and health concerns resurfaced, prompting me to reassess my career path once again. I told no one. Physically, the signs of declining breast health started showing up again. My doctor became very concerned.

When you're in senior management and being coached to be promoted, you should at least be aligned with the corporate culture and values, right? I believed that; however, I became clearly aware my values weren't aligned with the company's and that lack of alignment was at the root of my stress; which led me to resign giving a six-week notice without a plan or knowing my next step.

With my husband's support, he suggested taking two years off of stressful work to figure things out - get healthy and start a new career direction, just go for it. Inspired by the profound impact executive coaching had on my corporate life plus my interests in the career development field based on my past experiences, I decided to pursue career coaching as a profession.

I enrolled in the coach certification program at Career Coach Institute. I gained strong coaching skills, learned career techniques, and honed my networking skills. I was now ready to start my business.

My skills in project management, leadership, problem-solving, strategic planning, and building relationships were instrumental in launching my new venture as a Career Coach.

It took some time to come up with the right name for my business. Initially, I named it KEA & Associates, but since I didn't have any associates, I eventually settled on EnVision Career Design LLC. Through networking, I was fortunate to secure a career outplacement contract followed by another within a year.

I found great fulfillment in helping various professionals. As the years went by, I took on more contracts, leading to a growing workload. Additionally, I didn't just provide coaching; I also conducted training and facilitated career-related sessions.

I had the opportunity to coach individuals in a variety of industries, including the federal government, legal, tech, telecommunications, non-profit, manufacturing, and military, to name a few. My coaching spanned various levels of hierarchy, from C-Suite executives to those working on assembly lines, both within the US and internationally.

I felt much more fulfilled, and my health improved as well.

As time went on, I developed other interests too. Leadership coaching opportunities came my way, and I decided to obtain certifications as a BCC (Board Certified Coach), PCC (Professional Certified Coach), CGC (Certified Government Coach), Certificate as a Career Development Coaching Specialist, and trained as a Positive Intelligence Coach. I still love to learn, and I typically enroll in at least one training program each year.

What I realized a few years into the business was a need to keep my "Why" before me. I started to experience burnout - still healthy but overwhelmed.

That's when I developed "The 4F's©" motto, a principle that echoed the values I had learned from my family years ago in Denver and from just living life. I suggest every entrepreneur/solopreneur find their business guiding light principles and motto to help with their foundation while staying true to what is important to them.

This 4F's© motto has become and continues to be a guiding light for me:

- Freedom to be creative without constraints
- Flexibility of time for personal and professional endeavors
- Fun and enjoyable work
- Finances to exceed obligations with unlimited earning potential

Whenever the 4F's© are misaligned in the business, I know it is time to reassess and make changes. It usually shows up in decreased flexibility of time for me - along with unmet financial goals. This shows me it's time to raise rates, take on higher-paid contracts, shift my focus, or just take a short vacation break to reflect and look at the bigger picture. This approach has helped me stay aware and intentional. As a business coach once said: "Do Less, Better."

As I reflect on my path from that young girl in Denver attending summer school to the entrepreneur I have become, I've realized the value of having a clear vision and trusting in God's guidance. These lessons have been instrumental in helping me navigate the ups and downs of my career and life. And most of all, the significance of staying true to one's values.

My journey from corporate employee to entrepreneur is now a way of life for me. It's so natural and has been incredibly rewarding, enriching, challenging, and filled with valuable lessons - and still a bit of a balancing act for me. I have learned and practiced self-care, TAP (take a pause), resilience, and having a support system to help me become accountable to myself.

There are a few key takeaways from what I've learned and want to share:

- Learn to shift from an employee mindset to an entrepreneur mindset: Navigate uncertainty as a value rather than seeking a sense of security in a job.
- Prioritize self-care: Get clear on what self-care means for you, then incorporate it into your life, and take care of yourself.
- Value continuous learning: Invest in your craft, meet new people, and keep up with technology. Never stop seeking knowledge and new experiences.
- Maintain a clear vision: Take time to reflect, go deep, and constantly ask, "What do I want?"
- Develop a personal philosophy: Create your own motto - your guiding principles to help you make decisions and stay true to yourself.
- Be adaptable: The ability to pivot and adjust your course is crucial in today's dynamic work environment.
- Trust the process: Remember that entrepreneurship is rarely a straight path - be patient and persistent in this journey.

Each of these takeaways came from real-life experiences, whether it was overcoming a setback or seizing an opportunity that seemed daunting at first.

I hope that by my sharing my story with you, you will see that openness, commitment, and the willingness to pursue your goals can create wonderful possibilities and opportunities despite uncertainty, fear, and self-doubt. Just as my father encouraged me to gain real-world experience, I now encourage you to take action toward your vision to create the momentum forward.

Reflect on your life journey. Ask yourself over again, what do I want? Then ask:

- Where am I now? Is this where I want to be?
- What are my core values?
- How can I genuinely align my values with my professional life, business operations, and/or personal life?
- What one step can I "commit to" and "stick with" to move me closer to my vision today? Is there another step? What is it?

Remember, it's never too late to make a change or pursue a new direction. I hope my story has provided you with some inspiration and practical insights to pursue your passions, even to take steps to find fulfillment in your professional and personal life. Take care of yourself, stay true to your values, and trust the journey.

Thank you for taking the time to read about my journey. If you have any questions or would like to discuss your career path, please don't hesitate to reach out. I'm here to help and support you.

ABOUT KIM E. ANDREWS

Kim E. Andrews

Kim E. Andrews, CEO/Founder of EnVision Career Design, is a Board-Certified Coach and ICF-credentialed Executive Coach & Career Strategist with 20+ years of HR, leadership development, career coaching and mental fitness experience. She focuses on the whole person, empowering individual contributors and leaders to gain clarity and increase self-awareness to achieve their professional goals. Kim's dedication to her clients' success is evident in her ability to listen, understand, and offer fresh perspectives, helping them thrive in their professional journey. Drawing from her extensive background, Kim uses a high touch and high tech approach to deliver personalized coaching experiences.

Her commitment to measurable and meaningful outcomes ensures clients not only achieve their goals but also grow personally and professionally. Kim's holistic approach and deep expertise make her a sought-after coach for those looking to make impactful career transitions and develop strong leadership skills.

Website: www.envisioncareerdesign.com
LinkedIn: www.linkedin.com/in/kimeandrews

CHAPTER 4

Nicole J. Aspenson

NEVER STOP DREAMING

When I was seven years old, I had my first entrepreneurial venture: painting and selling pet rocks. My older brother and I also gathered golf balls that came over the fence from the country club where my dad lived. We sold them to other golfers. Nobody was looking, so no one could tell us we had an entrepreneurial spirit in our souls. It would take three decades for an awareness of my innate talents to blossom fully.

There was not much discussion in my family beyond the idea that you "should" go to college and get a great job. I wasn't told how to choose a good college or what kind of career path to pursue; I was left to discover that on my own.

I was what was called a "latchkey" kid. When we woke up in the morning, our parents were already gone - and we came home from school to an empty house. We got ourselves dressed, ready for school, on the bus, and home all on our own.

Even though I was the youngest of the two of us, it was often my responsibility to care for or help my parents with my brother, who had Type 1 diabetes, attending to the ever-present threat and frequent reality of insulin shock.

My dad was a success at his corporate job, but it wasn't enough. He had a bigger picture of success he wanted to attain. So, he formed a side hustle, creating a printing business. Even though he drove a BMW (an easy symbol for a child to equate with success), and even though he was accomplished and proud of what he had achieved, neither he nor my mother thought to suggest or discuss the options open for my brother and me. It never occurred to us that because our dad was a business owner, we could be too - never mind what that would take and what rewards and sacrifices would be involved. The very idea that there were ways of working other than trading time for dollars was inconceivable. It was only when I was 40 and I began to truly figure myself out that I discovered there were many more options available for a career and for my life.

On the outside, my childhood looked like that of many others: I attended gymnastics classes that I adored, spent time outside riding bikes and playing with friends, and was only required to go home when the streetlights turned on. However, on the inside, it was far less rosy than it appeared.

When I was five years old, my parents divorced. My mom had custody of us. She worked full-time and was also in school with a full course load, so her ability to be with us was limited. My grandmother offered my mother a lot of support and was willing to supervise us and watch out for our welfare. But she was older and had limitations; thus, we were mostly on our own.

An apocryphal lesson was presented to me years later as I watched my mom lose half of her 401(k) only two years before she was to retire. It would be another seven years before she was able to semi-retire - and at the age of 79, she still works part-time.

I had zero savings and thought I would work every day of my life with no retirement at all. I was not going to sign up for that plan for my elder years, but I had no clue yet how to avoid it.

Looking back, I see how my latch-key childhood served me: it gave me greater independence than my peers. It forced me to use my imagination to solve problems, and I developed the ability (out of necessity) to resolve conflicts with my peers. I discovered I held an adventurous curiosity. It kept me entertained and mostly out of trouble.

While in high school, I chose to go to cosmetology school at night. The plan was to make an income, as I had desired to go to college. My plan didn't work out as I had hoped, but I'll get to that in a little bit.

I graduated from cosmetology school and started a career at a retail hair salon, which I enjoyed. I was fortunate to work in a company that had a leadership development program. I had a manager whom I trusted and who respected me; she was my first mentor. I was promoted to Assistant Manager within the first year, Manager of my own store before the age of 24, and then General Manager of three stores by the age of 25. Without her support and mentorship, I'm unsure how I would have progressed so rapidly.

I got married and had a little boy. My son's father wanted to open a small business. I knew he would need help and knew I would need new skills to provide that help. I began taking classes, as they had provided a positive outcome in the past. This time, I went to develop accounting skills, to learn how to keep the books for a small business.

So, at the age of 25, I was a married "single mom," taking primary responsibility for raising our son while working a full-time job and doing bookkeeping for our business.

My husband and I struggled to have enough to pay for the rent and food, much less dream of a better future. I would roll up loose change and go food shopping. I took the list and a calculator with me to ensure there was enough money when I got to the register. Crying on my way home was my only release from the stress.

There were some good times. When our baby boy was born, it was a joy beyond measure. As he grew, the stress in my life grew. He was diagnosed with asthma when he was one year old. By the time he was two years old, it became a full-time job to keep him breathing.

My young son was then diagnosed with ADD, which required my being educated about the condition and how to help and support him. It turned out to be a truncated diagnosis; later, the diagnosis would be expanded to his being on the Autistic Spectrum. Remember, autism was not understood then as it is now.

Both my child's breathing and his brain were challenged, so there was no easy path there. Fortunately, during this period, we brought on a business investor, and I was able to resign from the salon and begin to work from home.

Being a survivor is a double-edged sword. I was surviving a complex and toxic marriage. There was the unending fear of ends not meeting, the inability to make my son well, and having nowhere to turn to see how to make it all work. Conversely, I had the strength to survive. As my awareness expanded beyond doing what I had to do, I looked inward. What I realized was that surviving was not enough: I wanted to thrive.

I lost myself, as many women do when juggling a career, family, school, and navigating the challenges life presents.
Facing the toxicity of my childhood and the damage that was done was not a skill I had developed. Like many people growing up in similar situations, I made choices that replicated those conditions as an adult; I knew nothing else. It took a long time to grow and to heal the damage done by living in survivor mode.

The time came to transition my son back into public school for high school. I decided to place him in a charter school. Sadly, with more than 24 percent of his class having special needs, it meant no one child truly got their individual needs met. After two years, and because I had control of my own schedule, I was able to pivot and enroll my son in an independent study program with another charter school. Finally, he could get the support he needed and succeed in school.

I had personal growth spurts that required determination. I transitioned out of my bookkeeping business in two years, and my son's father and I agreed that divorce would be the best for us both. Coming out of the divorce with a lot of debt, I could not pay my mortgage for several months without help from my parents. It was tough.

I needed to change the path I was on, take control of my destiny, deflate the toxicity in my life, and increase my income to create a sense of safety. The first step was remembering that nascent spark of self-governance when I sold painted rocks and reigniting it. I became my own boss. I launched a bookkeeping business; I was an entrepreneur! I could stay home and home-school my son.

In retrospect, I am amazed at how accustomed I had become to the stressors of life. I remain amazed and eternally grateful that years of want did not break my essential self - my spirit.
When my son graduated, he no longer needed me as much at home, freeing my time to grow my business, expand my skills, and find like-minded women with whom to network. I looked for opportunities during the daytime. I met a woman who told me she was in the financial services industry, which fascinated me. She invited me to an event to learn more.

Unfortunately, as I dug deeper into the company, I learned it was not in alignment with my values. They spoke about getting one person to sign up to make X dollars; if you got two people to sign up, you'd make X more dollars. They were not about helping others; it was never part of their discussions. I wanted to work with a company that focused on helping people. I knew that this would be my guiding principle and trusted I would find a company that aligned with what was important to me. So, I sought out other groups seeking different information and more answers. I started asking deeper questions.

I then got lucky and attended a small networking group called Wine, Women & Wealth®.

Imagine this: on my arrival, I saw ladies enjoying themselves, laughing with each other, checking in with each other's well-being, collaborating on ideas for connections, and doing business with a personal commitment to helping each other secure and keep good clients. This did not feel like a solely sales-based networking meeting! It intrigued me, and it felt like they were a good match for my values.

I wanted to learn more about the organization and its mission, which is: To guide women to financial success through education, support, and financial mentoring.
Yes, please!

This is a demonstration of how to empower and educate Main Street Americans about their money mindset and the basic principles of money we all should have learned growing up. I knew I had to be a part of this! At the time, I had no idea how much my income could grow. I found freedom in controlling my own schedule. However, I still hadn't learned about the idea of stopping the trading of time for money. My main goal was to help people! I started to gain hope.

Fortunately, I found a solution to that apocryphal lesson from my mom's retirement plan loss years earlier when I learned there are products to create "safe money." At that time, I had 30 years ahead of me for compound interest to start working in my favor. I thought I could show others that there were tools for financial freedom available.

Over the following months, I found remarkable leaders who cared about me and who saw more in me than I could ever imagine for myself. They offered training every week, where I learned about being successful in the financial industry. More importantly, I had a supportive, loving space in which to grow. This opportunity extended to my developing the strength and confidence to escape toxic environments and emerge from the financial struggle I had known all my life.

I was able to believe in myself again! I discovered it was much more fun being compensated for bringing value to clients and building my dreams instead of someone else's! I realized I could support myself and my son emotionally and financially. These leaders and mentors encouraged me to dive into personal growth to find myself, step into my power and passion, and be strong enough to hold space for other women to do the same.

Their Vision Statement Includes:

"It is the Dream of a place where the hurting, the frustrated, the disillusioned, and the confused can find love, acceptance, help, hope, guidance, and encouragement. It is a home for people that need a second chance or a third chance or however many it takes."

With persistence and consistency, only three years after the divorce, I made a six-figure income, was debt-free, and traveled on five-star reward trips and leadership retreats. About one year after my divorce, I felt ready to start dating, and I met the love of my life. He treats me with respect and kindness and gives me his unconditional love, providing immense support in business and in our personal lives.

I've been invited to speak as one of the top 20 agents at our national convention in front of hundreds of my peers. I've qualified for Continuing Education Academies and Leadership Retreats. I participated in events where hundreds of leaders gathered from around the country to sharpen their axes, share successful strategies, and collaborate with each other. My work is a place where we support each other and share what is working to create a successful business. More importantly, it always feels like a family reunion. There are lots of hugs and relationships built at these gatherings.

Through those Five-Star, all-expenses-paid vacations, I was able to take my new husband on our first vacation to St. Kitts. It was beyond anything I could have imagined. Later, we took an earned cruise to Alaska with friends and celebrated our engagement in a very special way. The following year, we went to Punta Cana, where we arrived for our early honeymoon, and then on to Las Vegas to drive super-fast race cars. I know there will be many more of these adventures in the future.

I also look forward to all the family reunions, with all of us gathering worldwide to be together.

Most importantly, I have been able to help over 250 families and business owners change their financial trajectory. Putting plans in place that include Living Benefits, a cash reserve in case of a major illness, tax-advantaged strategies, succession planning, creating a guaranteed lifetime income, and creating generational wealth.

The opportunity to help women take control of their finances - so that they will not feel stuck in any situation because they feel lost around money - excites me. I believe I was put here to encourage women to take charge of their money mindset and rewrite old stories that are not serving them. I am passionate about empowering and educating small business owners, women executives, and families about how money can work so they can obtain financial freedom!

Hosting Wine, Women, and Wealth® events - where we have vulnerable, heartfelt conversations about money and the money mindset with zero judgment - is a privilege, as is helping women find community, learn about money, and be encouraged and uplifted.

Yes, I found a home and family where I least expected. I connected with like-minded leaders who are passionate about being of service, whether it is for clients, fellow agents, or our community. I particularly enjoy giving people the tools to change their financial trajectory. I love inviting new business partners to come along on this journey with us, at whatever pace they need to be loved and supported. Finally, I love that we are a family that gets to change lives every day.

The financial services industry continues to grow and change, based on the economy and the needs of those they serve, not unlike most major industries. . I have seen products and services change dramatically over the past decade. I have seen corporate culture and responsibility up-level. Most exciting to me is that more women and younger generations are joining our industry and making a huge impact in business and in their own communities!

What I have learned is that the concept of work/life balance is misnamed. I believe in balance, though the scale will, by necessity, be tilted more in one direction or the other when you are focusing on a particular part of your life. The key is to find work/life harmony, work, friendships, personal development, joyful occupation, travel, and family.

My advice to young women who are exploring entrepreneurship starts with encouraging them to spend time identifying their core values and mapping out their dreams. Identify who you are and what you want out of your career. Pursue opportunities that align with your values. Be brave enough to try different opportunities until you find the right fit. Never give up on your dreams, goals, and passion; always be true to yourself. Always Dream!

I would encourage young women and men to find multiple mentors and coaches to guide them through their careers and lives. We all can benefit from both. Remember to seek out people who have already become successful in the area you want to pursue and about which you want to learn.

My life has changed dramatically since those days in the hair salon business. It may sound simplistic, but we must make mistakes, and we need to do the work for personal and professional growth before we can know true achievement. I am now an Executive Vice President and have been invited to speak of our work using my "Servant Heart" in Leadership and Mentorship roles. I have been rewarded for going through the muck, willingly trying and failing until I was able to find my place. I am continually rewarded through the culture, the community of people, and the company with whom I am associated. I know that is how my successes and that of my peers were endowed; we humbly stand on the shoulders of those who have come before, who have embraced and guided us.

We cannot succeed on our own. We cannot truly appreciate what we receive as our reward for hard work if we don't look down the road and see who we may next help, where we may best share, and how we can bring what we have become to those just starting out.

ABOUT NICOLE J. ASPENSON

Nicole J. Aspenson

Nicole J. Aspenson is an Executive Vice President with Five Rings Financial and the founder of Anchor Financial. She has a passion for helping her clients make smart financial decisions that they can feel confident about.

Nicole works with a range of clients; business owners, business executives, young families and successful singles to show them secure options for building and protecting their wealth.

Nicole is a speaker, author, safe money strategist, and living benefits expert. She hosts workshops like *Wine, Women & Wealth*®, where women support each other while learning about money, and Free Financial Literacy classes to educate on basic money principles.

Whether you want to take control of your finances or explore a career in helping others achieve their financial goals, connect with Nicole! Let's work together to make your financial dreams a reality.

Website: https://frfanchor.com/
Facebook: https://www.facebook.com/anchorfinanical
LinkedIn: https://www.linkedin.com/in/ncaplette/
Instagram: https://www.instagram.com/nicolejaspenson/?hl=en

Terri Beardsley

FROM SURVIVAL TO REVIVAL: TRANSFORMING LIFE ON YOUR OWN TERMS

My husband Sam said he wanted to go out to dinner tomorrow night after I got home from work. I didn't notice anything different from other times. We went to a local seafood restaurant we both liked, ordered wine and made small talk. When the wine arrived, we ordered dinner, that's when the bombshell hit. After 33 years together, Sam told me he wanted a divorce. He said he just wasn't happy, that wanted a quick divorce so we could get on with our lives. Since we were in a public place, I knew he expected me to hold it together and not make a scene. I was in shock that he would do this in the middle of a restaurant where people were enjoying a nice meal out. I could barely eat when our food came. All I wanted to do was leave and hide my face from everyone.

Facing divorce came as a shock, even though looking back I could see that there were problems. But I just chose to ignore them. I did not want to feel like a failure because my long-term marriage was not working, especially after more than three decades. Maybe I was being stubborn or thought that I was supposed to just tough it out as I was raised to do. After all, when I got married, I assumed that it would be for a lifetime. I did not want to be the one that dismantled my family. And luckily, I did not have to be, since my husband had asked for a divorce. That act, though shocking, freed me from having to make the decision. I realized that I was holding on because I was afraid to blaze a new trial for myself after feeling like I was not controlling my life for years.

Reflecting on my life, I see two pivotal leaps that reshaped my destiny. The first was when I was a young woman fresh out of high school. I joined the U.S. Air Force. Imagine me, a quiet girl from Virginia, stepping onto an airplane for the first time bound for an unknown future that would begin in San Antonio, Texas. I was full of excitement and trepidation, not sure what to expect. That leap took me west of the Mississippi and away from my family and friends, into a world where I had to stand on my own in a room full of strangers who would soon become friends. This was my initiation into a life of resilience, adaptability, and independence. I did not know it then, but the seeds of leadership would be planted in my heart during those four years of military service. Those seeds would remain below the surface for the next four decades until the time when they would be able to grow and guide me in a life of serving others through leadership.

While I was in the Air Force, I also met my future husband. It was a whirlwind romance that I realized too late was not as wonderful as I had thought it would be. We had a lot of good times, and he was able to get me to do some adventurous things that I would not have tried before. After a while life got in the way of enjoyment, and I ended up just surviving and letting him take control. After I got out of the Air Force, right after I had our first child, I had to find a job since my husband was in nursing school. It was a difficult decision to put a new baby in childcare and start a new job. I somehow did it and found myself a wife and new mother with a full-time job working for San Bernardino County. After he finished nursing school and worked for a bit of experience, he wanted to move from California to Oregon, where his family was, and where he grew up. We ended up selling our house and moving to Oregon, where I barely knew anyone - not even his family. I found out I was pregnant with our second child right after the move. The move was hard for me, I found myself spending most of my time with his family and our son., and not meeting many new people. After the birth of our second son, I started looking for a new job, as I was expected to work to help support the family.

I started working with the U.S. Postal Service when my second child was a year old. It was hard to have two children in childcare and work ridiculous hours as a new letter carrier. But somehow, I did it. I got up early in the morning ,took the kids to childcare and went to work, then picked the kids from childcare and came home to fix dinner.

That was my life for years. And when I had a third child, another boy, I somehow added sporting events and school activities to my day. When I look back, I cannot believe that I survived the crazy schedule. There were good times and travel mixed in. It was years before I realized that I was not happy with my life - but I did not know what to do about it. At that point I was so used to not being in control that I struggled to make choices when asked to do so. It was not until our kids grew up and left home that my husband decided it was time to split up.

The second pivotal leap in life was in the wake of my divorce. I had to confront fears that had lain dormant for years. I was forced to relearn how to be independent, self-sufficient, and happy in my own company. I remember my first public speaking engagement, a simple elevator pitch that felt like climbing Mount Everest. My voice trembled, my hands sweated, but I spoke and with each word the fear started losing its grip. That experience taught me a crucial lesson: the only way out of fear is through it.

During my marriage, Sam and I had trouble agreeing on many things. He was controlling and could be manipulative - and I would not fight against what he wanted. I found that it was just easier to go along. It took too much energy to deal with him. I was exhausted from all the things I was doing for him and our family while working full time and trying to keep the peace at home. I was tired, and not the kind of tired that you could just sleep off.

When I look back, I cannot believe that I let him have his way, that I just buried myself in my tunnel and let him have control over my life. Toward the end of my marriage, I found myself doing things behind his back to try and make things easier for myself and the family. I feel sad now that I couldn't see any other way. Since I could not win, I lost. I lost my identity, my voice, and my power. I lost my ability to stand up and command control of my life, I lost my relationship, and virtually everything I had known. But in losing all of that, I won. I won the ability to rebuild it all the way I wanted. And dealing with my fears was a big part of that rebuilding.

Have you ever felt lost in a relationship, and you did not know who you were or how you got there? So many of us have, and when you look back on the road to where you are, it can appear like a battleground. For me, it seemed like a familiar but uncomfortable wasteland where my dreams had all but died. I was crushed by what I did not see coming. The good news is that the road you have traveled does not have to be the road you keep traveling.

Another big part of my healing was becoming willing to share my story publicly. Three years ago, I shared my story at Confidence Catalyst, a first-time speakers' series. It was an amazing event that truly took me out of my comfort zone. It has taken me on a new journey that I would never have imagined myself taking. Speaking on this stage would become the catalyst for what was to come next in my life.

My talk was titled "My Journey from Tunnel to Passion," and it covered the 33 years of my life that I was married as well as the last eleven since I became divorced. I never thought that a marriage could end so abruptly, but it did, and I am forever grateful it did so. Why would anyone be happy that a 33-year relationship was over? How would I learn to live solo again? Thirty-three years is an entire lifetime for many people - and having to go back to square one at the age of 54 was not what I had envisioned in my life plan. Life plans aside, fate had something else in store for me, and boy did it.

The ending of that speech went like this: "We have traveled my journey and in conclusion I have realized how much I have grown in the last 11 years, as I have made a new life for myself. I am finally in a place where I can tell my story, and hopefully inspire others to stand up for themselves, no matter their age, so they can live the life they were meant to live. I have learned that I am called to help people in whatever way needed - and that has become my passion." I was so proud of that talk! It felt like a great recap of my life, but it was only the prelude.

A critical component of my journey of self-discovery following my divorce was embracing the power of community. I had never really had much of a community before, and it has become so important to me. In the early days post-divorce, I found solace and strength in a group of people who became my confidantes and cheerleaders. Together we navigated our new realities, proving that the bonds forged in adversity are unbreakable. This lesson in seeking and providing support has stayed with me as we enjoyed shared passions, from winetasting to wellness.

During this time, I was learning how to live on my own again. I had never lived in an apartment before. Luckily, I did not have to live in one extraordinarily long as our house sold, and I was able to start the process of looking for a new home. It was a scary process for me, as I had never done something like this on my own. Selling our property was another opportunity to stand up for myself. My ex-husband tried to do things his way, and we almost lost the sale - which was a cash offer! My realtor and I finally were able to get him to agree to a win-win outcome. This was a huge step for me as I learned to navigate my new life and have control over it.

One of the first things that I did after I moved into my own place following the divorce was to start running. I challenged myself to do a 5K race before I turned 55 - and I had less than six months to get ready. I had never been a runner, so this was something new for me. I had to figure out a routine that I could follow even though I was still working - and many days I worked overtime. I would go out every day after work and I kept running further distances until I could run the whole

5K distance. But unfortunately, two weeks before the race, I pulled my hamstring. I decided that I would do the race anyway, my oldest son and his fiancé ran it with me. I was not able to run the whole race, so I did a combination of running and walking.

I felt like I had made a major change in my life, I had not set goals for myself before this. And just so you know, I did run that race the following year with a friend.

I retired from the U.S. Postal Service a few years later. While it was not a decision I had planned to make at that time, I found the workplace so toxic that I had to leave. Since I was old enough and had enough years in, I went for it. It was scary, as I was still learning how to make decisions for myself that would affect how I would financially be able to live my life my way. It was an interesting time for me as I had no place I had to be, and I could do as I pleased. I had become a grandmother around that time, and it was an amazing experience to spend time with my granddaughter. I soon realized that I needed to find some other purpose in my life.

That led to my entrepreneurship opportunity. When a friend that I had worked with retired and decided to restart a business, she invited me to join her. I liked the company (called Life Vantage) and what the products could do for people, so I joined! I had never had a business before; this was a whole new experience for me. During this time my father, who lived in Virginia, started having more medical issues and I wanted to spend time with him while I was able to. I went to visit him a couple of times a year and we had some wonderful times together - times that I had not been able to have with my mother as she had died. My marriage and job plus having children at home didn't allow me to leave to be with her. But I still remember those times fondly and do not regret any of those trips.

After my father passed, I decided to get my business going and decided to try networking. I had no idea what I was doing - I had never even known much about it! I courageously stepped out of my comfort zone again and began putting myself out there for people to see. A whole new world opened for me, and I met so many new people who became my new community. I loved sharing about Life Vantage and how our products could help people.

Public speaking was something that terrified me. I stayed away from it for many years, until I had to stand up and do my elevator pitch. I stumbled many times, but through repeating it, I improved. When I had to give presentations, I had to keep to a script, or I could not remember anything. This was a major problem for me to overcome.

Speaking at Confidence Catalyst for the first time helped me realize that I could do public speaking. Since then, my life has taken turns that I would never have imagined before my divorce. I no longer hide, afraid of what people will think of me. I was vulnerable and told my story, I had nothing to hide any more.

I love supporting other women who may be experiencing similar issues and help them understand they can become whoever they let themselves become. It is not easy, but so worth it. And since many women are getting divorced later in life and are struggling to figure out what to do next, I want to be there for them to let them know they can make it. Their lives can be full of excitement and whatever they decide they want.

In January of 2020, I decided that I would spend the year working on myself. I started with mindset training. I had a coach for the first time in my life, I had to step out of my comfort zone yet again to share in a group setting. Little did I know that the Universe would help me by creating a situation that would keep me on a course that would change the way I lived my life. In March of that year everything shut down due to Covid19. It was a time that I spent a great deal of time reading books that could help me.

I also joined a mastermind group, an on-line Toastmasters group, a women's speaking club and a chamber of commerce. All of this was on Zoom, so I did not have to travel, which helped me be able to do it all. I learned a lot during this time and was able to establish habits that I still practice today. Establishing habits is something that you really must work at - it does not happen overnight. The changes you make take time to become habits, but once they become habits it becomes easier to do them regularly.

Some of the habits I have developed are ones that I started out small and added to until I was in the right place. I found that starting small and adding was the easiest way to develop habits that last.

One of the habits I developed is to have a to-do list that I complete every day., I have learned that if you make your to-do list too long you will get discouraged and quit doing it. Another new habit is I do 25 pushups daily. Doing pushups was something I learned in a book I read called Tiny Habits. The author recommends that you decide to do something and set a time or amount that you feel will work for you. If you accomplish what you decide would work, then you start developing a habit. You can always add on more, but the habit was the original amount. I started out doing five and worked my way up until I felt I had reached a good amount for me. The only time I do not do them is if I am sick or injured, which luckily has been only a few times. Other habits that I have developed are doing daily gratitude statements, affirmations, intentions, exercising, reading, and meditating. You do not have to spend a lot of time on each one, but just doing it helps you keep those habits going.

When I was given the opportunity to speak again, I was in a much different place than I was just three short years ago. I have stepped into my power, reclaimed my voice, and taken control of my life. This was a process that took several years, and a lot of soul searching. I am doing so many new things that I had never thought about doing. I have started hiking with a women-in-business hiking group, learned how to kayak with a friend, and modeled in several fashion shows. It is hard to believe that in the three short years between my talks, my life has taken so many leaps and bounds. It seems like it should have taken longer to achieve, considering how long it took me to get started.

Now I live life on my own terms. I say yes to things that may scare me, but at the same time will challenge me to try new things. I have said yes to taking on leadership roles, such as running meetings and doing presentations. This is not anything that I would have imagined myself doing. I am still amazed with all that I have overcome to get to a place where I can write a chapter in a book. This is something that is entirely new to me too - another first!

Why do I share these stories with you? Because each of us is standing at the edge of our own next leap. It might be the leap into a new career you have been dreaming of, the beginning or end of a relationship, or the pursuit of a long-buried dream. Whatever it is, know this: you are capable of more than you believe and stronger than you could ever imagine. So, I challenge you to identify one positive change you wish to make in your life. It does not have to be monumental. You could say yes to a new hobby you have been thinking about, reaching out to someone in need of a friend, or finally taking that dreaded public speaking class or workshop you have been avoiding, whatever it is, take that step. Embrace the uncertainty, the potential for failure, for in that space lies growth, transformation, and true living.

I invite you to reflect on your journey, to recognize the leaps you have already taken and to acknowledge the leaps yet to come. If a young woman from Virginia can find her wings in the Air Force, navigate the heartbreak of divorce at a later age, start her own business, and emerge to publicly tell her story yet again, imagine what you, with all your unique strengths and experiences can achieve?

Let us not leave our lives to chance, let us soar and make things happen on purpose. See what leaps you can make in your life by being willing to step outside of your comfort zone. In the end it is because of these moments of bravery that define us, that bring us to living life on our own terms.

ABOUT TERRI BEARDSLEY

Terri Beardsley

Terri Beardsley's personal and professional journey is a testament to the power of determination and growth. Serving in the Air Force instilled in her valuable skills and a strong sense of discipline. She then worked at the post office 31 years, which honed her organizational abilities and dedication to her community.

One of her pivotal moments, following an unexpected divorce after 30 years of marriage, was participating in a speakers' program in 2021 where she shared her personal story. Since then, she has embraced leadership roles and continued to break out of her shell, serving as committee chairs in the Tualatin Chamber of Commerce and a chapter co-director with the Women to Women Network. Beyond her professional endeavors, Terri finds joy in spending time with friends, exploring the outdoors through hiking and kayaking, and giving back to her community through volunteering with the Chamber and being on professional committees. Terri's commitment to family, community, and personal growth plays an important role in her life, inspiring all those around her to reach for their own aspirations.

Website: terribeardsley.lifevantage.com
Facebook: https://www.facebook.com/terri.b.beardsley
LinkedIn: https://www.linkedin.com/in/terri-beardsley-753a92175/

Carol Davies

TRANSITION FROM CORPORATE MANAGER TO CAREER COACH: MY MIDLIFE LEAP

One cloudy day in Geneva, Switzerland, I found myself loathing my job as a mid-level manager in a bustling office at the United Nations. The fluorescent lights hummed above my cubicle, and the air smelled of stale coffee and quelled ambition. But something gnawed at me - a yearning for more. While sitting through yet another monotonous PowerPoint presentation, it hit me like a lightning bolt: I craved autonomy. I wanted to shape my destiny, not just shuffle papers. So, I did what no sane person would do: I decided to quit. I gave my notice on the spot.

My colleagues gasped. "Carol, are you sure?" they asked. But I was resolute. Armed with determination and a laptop, I ventured into the world of career coaching.

This was an especially bold move for me to make, given my traditional background. And changing my career was not quite as straight-forward as you might think. I've navigated a transformative path from self-doubt to empowerment. And I've learned that you never know where life's going to take you! My story is one of resilience, growth, and unwavering belief in my worth. Let me take you through the pivotal moments that shaped my journey.

I received my undergraduate Bachelor of Arts degree in French and Spanish Literature from Western University located in my hometown. After completing my studies in the liberal arts, I initially had the idea that I would become a teacher or possibly a translator. (At that time, I didn't even know coaching existed as a profession.)

Upon further investigation, I found I had absolutely no interest in either teaching or translating. Instead, I decided my career goal was to become a professional librarian. I then decided to study for a master's degree in library and information sciences. Writing and conducting research in my new area of study was a perfect match for me. I finally knew where I was going.

When I finally landed my first job in Ottawa, Canada, I wasn't exactly the most daring person in the world. My birthplace was London, Ontario, a city of medium size, and I remained a resident of my hometown until I turned 25 years old. My only sibling is my twin sister. Since I am a twin, I always saw myself as part of a unit. My sense of self-identity was not particularly strong at the time. My family and I enjoyed a stable home life. My father worked full-time, as did my mother. With mother not being a stay-at-home mom, my sister and I were accustomed to being self-sufficient.

And so, I began my professional life as a librarian in Ottawa, Canada. I never imagined that I would eventually become a coach. I mistakenly thought that coaches only worked with athletes! My career took me down paths I didn't initially consider. I had obtained my qualifications as a librarian and information specialist in Canada. I held two interesting positions in Ottawa, where I lived for five years.

I first worked for three years as a librarian at the National Library of Canada and later for two years as a technical information manager at a transportation research non-profit organization (Transportation Association of Canada). I really enjoyed both positions. When I was working on special projects, I had the opportunity to travel internationally. This was such a motivating experience that I started thinking about widening the scope of the types of organizations for which to work so I could travel internationally more often.

I left Canada in 1981 to live and work in New York. This marked the beginning of my career in the corporate business arena. I was hired for special projects as a librarian at a prominent international consulting firm (McKinsey and Company). I was so excited. My dream of working internationally was coming true.

Believe it or not, I experienced culture shock. My adjustment from living in Canada to living in New York was not easy. Once again, I felt I had to abandon my family and friends. I was starting over again. However, to advance in my profession I decided it was time for me to take this new opportunity. It was during the relocation that I had my first experience working as an expatriate (often known as an "expat").

For a long time, I thought the cultures of the United States of America and Canada were rather comparable. For example, when it comes to the use of English, there are significant disparities. There is American English, Canadian English, British English, and so on. I felt different and like I didn't fit in. It took a long time to develop a supportive group of friends and activities in New York. I struggled with starting over yet again.

When I was 30 years old, I was recruited to work for the United Nations in New York. Over the 22 years I was employed there, I worked first at its headquarters in New York and then at its European headquarters in Geneva. In fact, it was a unique opportunity where I worked in a multicultural environment of ambassadors, diplomats and staff members from countries around the world. I worked as the library database manager for nine years at its premier library, the Dag Hammarskjold Library. I got excellent opportunities to do training and presentations at group seminars. In 1992, I transferred to the United Nations Library in Geneva, Switzerland, where I spent 14 years. Over the course of my career, I was very fortunate to acquire skills in technical applications for information systems as well as outstanding management training.

While I worked at the United Nations, I had always provided informal guidance or advice to my coworkers regarding their professional aspirations and growth. People sought me out for ideas, encouragement, and suggestions regarding how to acquire the job they want or how to plan their career path. This happened naturally. I enjoyed assisting them in filling out their job applications and writing outstanding resumes and curriculum vitae. This gave me validation that I was a natural coach. So, in 1999, I made a career move and started working for a different United Nations agency called the Joint Inspection Unit. That unit oversees conducting external audits of all institutions inside the United Nations system.

I was given the role of information system officer. I was a member of a team that was responsible for planning the successful transition to the year 2000 for the organization. - and it was not a good match for either my abilities or my goals.

Then in the early 2000s, I started feeling restless. I found that my career in the United Nations no longer fulfilled my dreams and aspirations. It felt like every day was just more of the "same old, same old." When you are older and working for the United Nations, there are far fewer opportunities for career development or change. There is a strong emphasis on tradition and hierarchy within the United Nations. People are frequently hired on contracts that are just for a brief period, and there is intense rivalry for positions.

I made the decision to quit the United Nations and give my notice at the end of 2005. Because I had deeply appreciated working as an international public servant, it was a challenging choice to decide to leave. So why did I make the leap to career coaching?

Reason #1: **Freedom**
I craved freedom - the kind that didn't come with vacation days or approval chains. My business idea? A career coaching practice. No more spreadsheets; just conversations, insights, and dreams.

Reason #2: **Impact**
Corporate life felt like pushing pebbles uphill. But as a coach, I could create ripples. I'd guide professionals toward clarity, confidence, and purpose. Impact mattered.

Reason #3: **Passion**
Corporate ladders led to glass ceilings. My passion? Helping others climb. So, I traded my heels for empathy, my Outlook calendar for personalized plans. The boardroom became my canvas, and self-discovery my currency.

In my mid-50's, I wanted to investigate what it was that I truly desired to do with the second half of my life. My professional life was no longer allowing me to follow my dreams and achieve my goals. When I was ready, I was prepared to return to the private sector. I posed the question to myself, "What is it that I would most like to do?"

I had a strategy in mind. I didn't just up and quit without any warning. I had completed the training for coaching. I studied at night via teleseminars at Coach U. It was a leap of faith, fueled by the fire within. I left the UN but stayed for another year in Geneva.

The day I handed in my badge, I hugged my colleagues - and I stepped into the unknown.

With a plan in hand, I didn't leap blindly. I had already completed coaching training, ready to guide others as they navigated their own crossroads.

The first week, I stumbled over coaching frameworks. The second week, I found my rhythm. Entrepreneurship was a rollercoaster, but I clung to the handlebars.

Word spread faster than recommendations on LinkedIn. Carol's Passion Motivator Coaching Haven became a local sensation. Professionals sought me out for résumé revamps, interview prep, and career pivots. I'd never been happier.

I had always been passionate about helping others achieve their full potential. In Geneva, Switzerland, I built an initial successful coaching practice focused on empowering women to overcome their challenges and thrive in their personal and professional lives. However, as I looked around at the women entrepreneurs in Geneva and the surrounding area, I couldn't ignore the overwhelming stress and burnout that seemed to plague so many of them. Sadly, it proved too expensive to live and work in Geneva. I decided to return to Canada and establish my coaching practice in the Toronto area.

I was driven by a desire to make a difference on a larger scale. Again, I made a bold decision to leave my familiar surroundings and travel to Canada to start a coaching business specifically tailored to help stressed, busy women entrepreneurs. With a sense of excitement and determination, I packed my bags and embarked on a new chapter of my coaching journey.

Upon arriving in Canada, I was met with a series of challenges that tested my resilience and determination. The cultural differences, unfamiliar business landscape, and competitive market made it difficult for me to establish myself in this new environment. In addition, I quickly realized that the mindset and struggles faced by the women entrepreneurs in Canada were different from those I had encountered back in Switzerland. Despite these obstacles, I remained committed to my mission of supporting women entrepreneurs in Canada. I immersed myself in the local community, attended networking events, and reached out to potential clients to understand their unique needs and challenges. Through these interactions, I gained valuable insights into the aspirations, fears, and motivations of the women I sought to help.

As I began working with my first Canadian clients, I discovered a common thread among them - a deep sense of overwhelm and exhaustion. The women entrepreneurs I met were juggling multiple roles, striving for perfection in every aspect of their lives, and sacrificing their own well-being in the process. I realized that to truly help these women, I needed to address not just their professional goals, but also their personal struggles and self-care practices.

In my coaching sessions, I encouraged my clients to prioritize self-care, set boundaries, and delegate tasks to alleviate some of the stress and pressure they were experiencing. I introduced mindfulness techniques, stress management strategies, and time-blocking methods to help the clients create a sense of balance and regain control of their lives.
As I continued to work with these women entrepreneurs, I witnessed their transformation unfold before my eyes. I saw the women let go of perfectionism, embrace self-compassion, and make room for joy and fulfillment in their lives. The women I coached began to experience greater clarity, confidence, and resilience in navigating the challenges of entrepreneurship while maintaining a sense of well-being and balance.

Through my early experiences in Canada, I learned many valuable lessons that would shape my coaching practice and personal growth. I learned the importance of adaptability, perseverance, and cultural sensitivity when working with clients from diverse backgrounds. The power of empathy, active listening, and authentic connection in building trust and rapport with my clients was paramount.

Among those lessons are:
1. **Resilience**: When clients doubted themselves, I lifted them up. When setbacks came, I adapted. Coaches thrive on resilience.
2. **Community**: My clients became allies. We dissected job descriptions over virtual coffee. Business wasn't just about profit; it was about transformation.
3. **Balance**: I worked harder than ever, but it was my passion. I danced between coaching calls and content creation, and it felt right.

It's a common dream for those working a corporate job to switch things up and start making an online income for themselves. Not many attempt to do so, and even less find success. So, what separates those that can with those that can't?

A lot of the challenges that I met in life involved having feelings of never totally being worthy of love, recognition, or financial success. I projected a strong, confident outer mask, but inside I felt like a very scared, small child looking for validation from outside sources. I put on this wonderful persona that all was well in my world, but inside a lot of the times I was just lost and afraid.

When I'd established my new coaching company in Canada, it seemed to take much longer than anticipated for my business to be noticed or to get clients easily. I became aware of some troubling thoughts I felt were holding me back. I worried I wasn't good enough. I told myself I don't have what it takes to be successful and I'm going to get found out. I discovered I was experiencing all the fears I was helping clients with: I felt like a fake, an imposter. It's called imposter syndrome and is very often experienced by new women entrepreneurs.

I felt like an imposter in my own success story. I heard a nagging voice whispering, "You don't belong here," even when external evidence suggests otherwise. As a new woman entrepreneur who embarked on this rollercoaster journey at the tender age of 55, I've grappled with these feelings firsthand. But fear not, fellow trailblazers! Let's delve into the incorporation theory of imposter syndrome and discover how to conquer it.

Imposter syndrome wears many masks: self-doubt, perfectionism, overwork, and the perpetual fear of being unmasked as a fraud. It's like attending a masquerade ball where everyone else seems to know the dance steps, and you're stumbling in borrowed shoes. But here's the secret: acknowledge those feelings. Name them. Say, "Hello, Imposter Syndrome, old friend." By doing so, you strip away its power, revealing it for what it is - a phantom menace.

I would start each day with great intentions about what I was going to do to promote my business - potential clients to connect with, content to share, and offers to make. Yet at the end of the day, I was flooded with shame and disappointment as I hadn't done any of those things, because they're too hard, too scary - out of my comfort zone.

I downplayed my achievements. I chalked them up to luck or assumed anyone could have done the same. But pause! I had to put myself in the place of my clients and say to myself, "You've climbed mountains, crossed treacherous bridges, and built your castle brick by brick. You belong here!" I made a list of my accomplishments - both big and small. Did I land that client? Celebrate! Did my website go live? Pop the virtual champagne! I reviewed this list regularly, like a weekly rendezvous with my proudest moments. I shared them with a trusted confidante who cheered me on.

I had to reframe what I saw as failures. Failure isn't a tombstone; it's a stepping stone. Imposter syndrome magnifies our missteps, whispering, "See? You're not cut out for this." But by framing it, I could imagine my failures as chapters in my entrepreneurial saga. Each one teaches resilience, adaptability, and the art of rising from ashes. So, when that project flops or the pitch falls flat, channel your inner phoenix. Dust yourself off, rewrite the script, and emerge stronger. Failure isn't final; it's fertilizer for growth.

Also, I realized I wasn't alone. I sought allies. I wasn't like Frodo on a solo quest to Mordor in Lord of the Rings. I connected through business networking with fellow entrepreneurs - the Gandalfs, Aragorns, and Samwises of my journey. I shared my fears, swapped battle scars, and learned from their sagas. They've faced imposter syndrome too, and their wisdom is your elixir. I attended networking events and joined online communities. Remember: vulnerability isn't weakness; it's your superpower. Together, we slay dragons (and imposter syndrome). I've achieved my objective of being a career coach for women entrepreneurs, my dream profession. And it's my fondest wish that you will too!

Being an entrepreneur isn't a linear path. When imposter syndrome whispers, "You're not enough," rewrite the script. Declare: "I am enough. I am the protagonist of my tale, flawed but fierce." And guess what? Every hero stumbles, but they rise, sword in hand, ready for the next chapter.

So, I learned to embrace my imposter syndrome. It's the spice that flavors your narrative, the dragon you'll eventually tame. Dance with it, learn from it, and remember you're not an imposter; you're a creator, a dreamer, and a force to be reckoned with. Now go forth, my fellow entrepreneur, and conquer galaxies. Your cape awaits!

ABOUT CAROL DAVIES

Carol Davies

Carol Davies is CEO and the career success strategist at Passion Motivator Coaching since 2007. She helps busy, stressed women professionals find a way to leave the corporate world to become a successful entrepreneur. She helps clients clarify what they really want to do in their personal and professional life. Her programs help clients create and achieve the life that they've only just dreamed about. They learn ways to find their true passion in life, to get a life plan with solid goals and a roadmap to achieve success.

Carol offers online group coaching and specialized courses to help clients clear resistance to change and get the life they have only dreamed of. She uses a mixture of holistic modalities such as life coaching, NLP, EFT (Emotional Freedom Technique) Tapping, and Reiki with her clients. Carol's philosophy is "Happiness is a choice to be the best you can be."

Website: www.thepassionmotivator.com
Facebook: www.facebook.com/Caroldaviesthepassionmotivator
LinkedIn: www.linkedin.com/caroldaviesthepassionmotivator
Instagram: www.instagram.com/thepassionmotivator
Website: https://femalefoundersgrowthacademy.com

CHAPTER 7

Dr. Mindy Gewirtz

DR. MINDY'S 7 SECRETS: LIVING AN ADAPTIVE WORKLIFE

"Mommy," I screamed, "I can't move my leg!"

I woke up in bed, terrified. I couldn't move my left leg. It lay paralyzed on the bed. My mother had this frightened look on her face. She wrapped me in my blanket and ran to the doctor's office. The nurse had seen this before. A raging polio epidemic gripped the country in the early 1950's. Dr. Jonas Salk developed the polio vaccine. I was ready for use in April 1955. Before the vaccine, victims of polio could lay trapped in an iron lung (a mechanical respirator that enclosed a child's body from the neck down). Others walked with the help of braces and crutches for the rest of their lives, like a member of my extended family.

I was four years old. I am forever grateful to the Almighty for having been spared. My case of polio was mild, and the vaccine had just become available. I was under a doctor's care for several years, and my leg had to be exercised daily to teach it to walk again. Many of us experience some form of trauma (with a small "t") growing up. The experience of polio left me with deep-seated doubt about my capacity to stand on my own two feet - literally.

Growing up as the child of two holocaust survivors, little traumas were a normal part of life. Both parents were fortunate and grateful to be alive and live in the United States. However, their trauma - losing their parents, grandparents, siblings, great-grandparents, and their extended families - was costly. They lost their homes, their wealth, and their standing in the community. Most of all they lost their physical health and struggled with their mental well-being. We didn't know about PTSD in the 1950's - but that was what they and others experienced.

Research shows that children of survivors, as we are labeled, have epigenetically acquired the stress, the anxiety, and the fear, that our parents had. Many of us - myself included - didn't have easy childhoods. We were caregivers to our parents. We grew up in the shadow of unpredictability, afraid that the good life could come and be taken away at any time, even if we did nothing wrong. We lived with the uncertainty of our parents' health. Research shows that holocaust survivors age prematurely by about ten years.

I knew I didn't have a lot of toys or clothes or go on many trips, but neither did many of the other children of survivors. I felt rich because we always had a lot of good food to eat. My mother never wanted us to experience the hunger she did in the concentration camp. I had lunch at a classmate's house in sixth grade, and remember to this day, her mom reminded her: "Take only one slice of American cheese for your sandwiches, okay?" I wanted to cry, and not take food out of their mouths. I also didn't want to embarrass her. I intuitively knew her family was on a tight budget. We were too, but never about food. To this day, like my mother, I always have a lot of food on hand.

The school became my escape zone. There I excelled, and by sixth grade, I knew I would attend college, unlike many of my peers. I blossomed in the all-girls Judaic and English studies high school. I enrolled in Brooklyn College with a full scholarship to cover books, because we couldn't afford them. I simultaneously attended a women's teacher's seminary, graduating with a Judaic teacher's license. After completing seminary, I took a job teaching afternoons at a Hebrew School to earn money and contribute to the household.

These early experiences built a library of limiting beliefs. In the darkest moments, I could have succumbed to the anxiety and sadness of life's challenges. Yet somehow, I absorbed my mother's incredibly adaptive spirit and resilience of mind.

- Negative forces restrained me from asserting myself and finding my voice. Foremost a caregiver, I took care of everyone else.
- A parallel energy source within me fueled my desire to be independent, support myself, and not rely on others. College was the first step and I was the first graduate in our family. My dream was to become a clinical psychologist.
- Perhaps having more control over my life where I had no control was part of the driving force. I became adept at unlearning and learning new methods, attracted to the forefront of knowledge and innovation, never in the moment, always facing the future.

I met my husband at 19, and we married the following year. My husband finished his master's in education and his Rabbinic ordination degrees. I sped up my college journey, graduating six months early. I picked up my Phi Beta Kappa pin waddling down the aisle, five months pregnant. I was unaware at the time that we were having twin boys.

Two days after we found out we were having the twins we moved to Virginia to our first congregation. I worked feverishly for 48 hours to put our two-bedroom duplex in order. That night I went into labor and met my doctor for the first time, at the delivery. The identical twin boys were the first in the family. We celebrated with extraordinary joy. A year later our eldest daughter was born. We had a ready-made family of three children in two years. And they all shared the exact birthdate.

"Join the Rabbinate, see the world," people said. After two years in Virginia, the congregation in Monticello New York offered my husband a larger position. Our second daughter was born there. I traveled to New York City (NYC) on Sundays for two years to earn a Master's in Gerontology. The master's degree maintained my NYC teacher's license, which I earned with my BA.

We moved three years later for a more prestigious Rabbinic position in Albany NY, where our third son, our fifth child, was born. My husband started a PhD program in Education Administration. I left teaching elementary school, since I saw very few women moving into administration. My goal was to make a difference bigger than one class at a time. The following seven secrets mark my progress.

SECRET ONE:
LIVE AN ADAPTIVE LIFE THAT WORKS FOR YOU

Becoming a psychologist, my initial dream, would take too many years and be too expensive. But by earning a social work degree, I could work and earn more quickly, without the dreaded dissertation. With five children under the age of seven, and my responsibilities as the wife of a Rabbi (a different story), my husband and I decided together that I would go the four-year part-time route.

I earned a scholarship to attend the MSW program at SUNY Albany. Then the surprise game-changer happened. I won the Max Siporin scholarship for $2,000 for two years. In 1979, $2,000 covered the rest of tuition and babysitting expenses. The other children were already in school. I decided I could manage the household, go full-time, and finish the program in two years. So I decided that I would move forward with the plan. However, sharing my exciting surprise award and plan right before going to sleep turned out to be an unmitigated disaster.
My husband's expression told it all. We had agreed on a plan, and I just blew it up without his input. "Maybe you want to think this whole thing through again," he said gently.

I knew he didn't like to be blindsided like that. He worried it would be too much for us. He did have an excellent point. It was a little crazy. In hindsight, I have no idea how we managed, considering I was attending school, studying, drafting papers, and running a household. We were typically good at working things out, but not that night. I went to sleep angry, mostly at myself, for not finding my voice, and presenting a compelling case of how we could manage it and what I meant by that.

My husband surprised me the next day with a beautiful bouquet of red roses. I didn't like roses, but I knew he was saying he cared. I didn't recognize how the anger welled up from the depths of my soul and suddenly found its voice. "I don't want flowers," I cried. "I need your help." I took the flowers, marched into the kitchen, and unceremoniously dumped them in the garbage can, smashing the delicate petals. I didn't want to be tempted to take them out again later.

This experience marked a milestone in our lives. We evolved from traditional roles to adaptive ones that worked for our new stage in life. It was the 1980's. I still had the primary responsibility for the household. My husband, an involved father, always helped whenever he could. What I wanted - but couldn't articulate clearly - was a change in our modus operandi. I finally got the compelling case clear in my head. I wanted us to be intentional and adaptive in figuring out how we manage the household together. We would plan things together ahead of time, rather than assume that I, as the traditional stay-at-home mom and the primary caregiver, would be responsible for everything. We now understood each other and created guidelines that worked for us. We agreed I would go full-time for one semester and assess how we managed.

We had a simple North Star for our guideline:
- Our marriage, family, and faith came first.
- School, the synagogue, and careers came second, third, or fourth depending.

Reflecting today, I understood that dropping the bomb when I did and deciding without his input wasn't wise. I know now to watch my passion and impulsivity. I also learned that the pilot project concept of trying out one semester and revisiting our decision was useful for us. We committed ourselves to making the new guidelines work for our family.
Creating this new adaptive life was transformative. I thrived in graduate social work school. Exhausted from the long hours, I still had more

energy than before. We loved shopping together once a week, as it gave us precious alone time. We became more efficient at household management. I cooked meals on Sundays to make the week easier. My husband took care of laundry (I folded and put it away), errands, and finances. He didn't cook, but I never ran those pesky errands I call the "time ankle biters." And I still don't do them today unless I must.

The first semester was tough, but we were committed. I earned a master's in social work in two years and went on for licensure. My first position at the Ringel Institute of Gerontology and my work there with my colleagues led me to become an Associate author of the book Elderly Criminals. In my next position at the Jewish Family Service agency in Albany, I saw clients and coordinated the eldercare service department. Six years later the executive director of the agency and I were set to apply for our PhDs together.

But we were on the road again. This time the largest Orthodox congregation in New England chose my husband as their Rabbi. My career had blossomed in Albany, so leaving was bittersweet. My executive director in Albany reached out to the director of the Jewish Family Service agency in Boston and recommended that she hire me - whether a position was available or not.

I was 34 years old and still afraid to swim because I had gotten the polio virus from the lake we played in as a little girl. I never learned to ride a bike and avoided driving as much as possible. I didn't trust my left leg because it had suffered from polio, which resulted in the loss of one-half inch of growth. Yet despite all my ingenious attempts to hold me back, an equally compelling force drove me forward. I had this burning fire to forge a positive impact in the world and realize the potential other people saw in me. I finally realized that potential in Boston.

We settled in a beautiful suburb of Boston. The women were excited to have me there. They heard stories about my twins playing in the playpen while I helped the women cook 350 meals for the annual dinner. The sisterhood couldn't wait for me to take on projects, participate in meetings, and take over as Sisterhood President. Attending night meetings after a full day of school and/or work and cooking dinners for 300 people was the furthest thought from my mind.

I understood the twofer expectation from the older women, which held that a Rabbi's wife should volunteer her time - even though we were in the 1980s and 1990s. She was expected to be a host for families on the weekend, run programs, attend meetings, give classes, and generally fill in the gaps where there was a need. Surprisingly, even younger women who philosophically aligned with work/life balance and gender equity in pay and other areas, made an exception when it came to the Rabbi's wife. This has evolved over the past three decades, and most Rabbi's wives now work outside the home, and many have advanced degrees. There is less of an explicit expectation by the community. However, even today, the engaged Rabbi's wife is an unspoken asset to her husband when applying for a position.

Boston became our home and community for 30 years and we loved it. I found my voice there. I started an organization within the fold of the synagogue women. Its mission was devoted to acts of kindness to members of our congregation. We ran on a network basis and rarely met. We divided into two pods, one to help women the week after they gave birth and one to help families for the week after the funeral at the end of life. This financially self-sustaining program has run for 30 years primarily by the younger women and continues today. I wrote grants for programs, founded a cross-community matchmaking service, counseled, entertained, navigated politics, and practiced diplomatic services. Some people thought I was an exceptional role model and were proud when I won a national award. Others in the community thought I never did enough.

My inner voice grew stronger over the decades. I no longer relied on external validation and recognition that did or didn't come. By day I loved working in the nonprofit family service agency as a leadership team member and in my private therapy practice. I founded my first external nonprofit organization, The North American Network for Jewish Information Services, and the article I wrote about the network appeared in the Journal of Jewish Communal Service. My entrepreneurial spirit blossomed creating innovative and financially profitable programs that were unheard of at the time. I charged the children and not the elderly for a suite of long-distance caregiving services, including assessment with a nurse, case management, therapy, and ongoing coordination of care.

I began and finished my coursework for a joint PhD program at Boston University in three years. I thought my thesis would be on holocaust survivors as they age. As a joint program, I could take courses in the business school. My experience there with like-minded entrepreneurial students or those with corporate experience was transformational. I found people in the program who understood the entrepreneurial part of me. I loved learning about leadership, change, adaptability, and working on group projects to create change. My dissertation focus shifted to work/life issues - specifically eldercare benefits and policies. The research was conducted in the large insurance company The Travelers Companies (later bought out by IAG) and studied the impact on people who used their benefits.

My entrepreneurial drive to have an impact at the individual, team, and organizational levels grew stronger. Wherever I have gone, I have challenged the norms. Whether living an adaptive worklife, designing my role in the congregation, carving out an entrepreneurial niche in a family service agency, or even conducting research for my dissertation, why was I always ahead of the curve?

SECRET TWO:
PHOENIX RISES FROM THE ASHES

"The synagogue is burning. The synagogue is burning."
I found the man shouting on my porch, with tears in his eyes as I opened the front door to my old Victorian home. We all went into shock. The synagogue had burned to the ground in the middle of the night. No one knew why or how it happened. People had gone to early minyan (sunrise prayers). One person ran into the fire risking his life to save several holy Torahs (scrolls). Everything else went up in flames, including the prayer books, the wooden pews, and the wooden Ark that held the scrolls. Charred bits of paper remnants, carefully collected for ritual burial, reminders of decades of memories were all that remained. The silver decorations for the scrolls melted down to nothing in the heat of the fire. The FBI investigated. It wasn't arson or a hate crime. It was an electrical

fire. People came piling into our house for morning prayers. The police, the firefighters, the journalists were everywhere. Chaos, grief, and shock gripped our community.

Coincidentally, that very same morning I had my full dissertation committee from both departments of the dual degree review my first draft. I must have smelled from the intense smoke. The hearing turned into a conflagration and chaos worse than the fire. It took months of rewriting, but we finally got the dissertation in shape to everyone's satisfaction on both sides of the committee. The lessons I learned about navigating educational organizational politics were painful enough to keep me from becoming a faculty member for two decades. I had learned diplomatic skills and emotional regulation as a Rabbi's wife. Navigating organizational politics comes with a diplomat's credentials - but university politics between social work and sociology departments regarding research methodology and faculty rights versus their dean was a whole new level for me.

I finally walked down the aisle to receive my doctoral diploma in a red cap and gown, two years after my husband earned his. I acknowledged thanks to the Almighty and shared my degree with my mother and her mother and grandmother who were all with me that day, as they never had a chance to live out their dreams. When I walked back down the aisle, my husband presented me with a bouquet of red roses. I still don't like roses; however, this time I graciously accepted them. I could never have survived the dissertation process without his unwavering support.

The synagogue building was rebuilt with much drama. Research shows that most houses of worship that burn down in a fire do not get rebuilt. I can understand why. This story is for another time. The famous architect Graham Gund designed the beautiful building, and by a miracle, we were back in it within two years. I continued rising, adapting, and learning on campus in business and life.

SECRET THREE:
PRACTICE MENTAL FLEXIBILITY AND POSSIBILITIES WILL SHOW UP

And the wheel of life spins again. I met Aaron Feuerstein, president of a $500 million textile mill in Massachusetts. He took an interest in my career. He was a proponent of giving women opportunities. His wife was a champion of childcare and worker benefits. Though I was still working at Jewish Family Services, he asked me to build a childcare center at his mill - and I said no. I gave compelling reasons why not and suggested a proposal more suited to his diverse workforce. One thing led to another, and I found myself consulting at the mill one day a week, on my day off. I loved social work, helping people through therapy, and implementing innovative programs. What I loved even more was accelerating the impact of change on individuals, teams, and organizations.

After working there for a decade, I resigned from Jewish Family Services. They knew I was pursuing leadership, coaching, and organizational consulting at the mill and wished me well. We ate cake in the agency conference room and hugged goodbyes. I left that day, and I never looked back. I knew I would always carry the therapist within me. I will always have the heart, care, and compassion of my faith as a leader.

I said goodbye to downtown Boston where I worked, goodbye to the legendary Filene's Basement where I shopped, and goodbye to my corner office.

The entrepreneur in me overcame the fear, the uncertainty, and the unpredictability of having no experience, business acumen, or financial backing. "Build it and they will come," from the movie Field of Dreams, became my business motto.

Working with Aaron Feuerstein and the textile manufacturing mill, I recognized I needed more resources for the expanding projects. I joined GLS Consulting as an equal Partner. One of the partners had been my mentor in my two-year post-doctorate certificate (HROD), the Human Resources Organizational Development Program. (Did I mention that continuous bleeding-edge learning of the field is my superpower?)

Once my partner was aboard and I was free from a four-day workweek at the agency, my brain ran free to innovate. We surveyed the mill's workers and managers. We spoke to childcare providers in the community where the mill was located. We got buy-in from the Union. We wrote an incredible proposal and were ready to present it on a Friday morning.

SECRET FOUR:
KINDNESS AND GRATITUDE BOOMERANG BACK

That same day, a small fire broke out at the mill. The $100,000 dedicated to the childcare project blew up in smoke. However, we communicated regularly with the workers and earned their trust. We developed a strong relationship with the head of Human Resources and Employee Relations, and they kept us in the loop.

A while later, we heard the mill was changing into a 24/7 operation, meaning overtime would be gone, a precious perk in the union seniority system. The union leaders started to talk about a strike. I marched into the President's office wearing my red dress with big gold buttons. I hovered over his desk with all the confidence my 5'2" frame could muster (channeling Madeleine Albright) and smacked my hand on the table to get Aaron's attention.

"Aaron, workers are getting ready to strike. Flyers are being distributed in the parking lot," I said. Luckily, I had done my research beforehand. I knew that a nationally renowned shiftwork expert lived in the Boston area. I had read his book and spoken to him. He was willing to meet Aaron. I suggested the following to Aaron: "Bring an expert on shiftwork to give people choices among the diverse types of shift work schedules. This is what the research says is effective. When people vote for their schedule, they are less likely to resist. If you force a particular shift work schedule, you could unintentionally hurt the most vulnerable people. Let me put together a joint management and union Hardship Committee to ensure that every person who needs consideration because of a medical or mental vulnerability will get consideration regardless of their union seniority."

Aaron did just that - and the strike was averted at the eleventh hour. The workers chose the best shift work schedule possible. We facilitated the first-ever joint union-management committee, and no union grievance occurred. A month after the new schedules gained footing, workers reported that there was no way they would go back to the old schedule.

Then came the catastrophic fire that burned down the most lucrative facility in the mill. Aaron could have retired as a very wealthy man by taking the money offered by the insurance company. All he had to do was let go of 3,000 workers in the middle of the winter and shut down the mill.

Aaron chose instead to pay his workers through the harsh winter months and rebuild the mill. The workers adored him. He saved people's jobs and the town. The media called him the "mensch (person of integrity) that saved Christmas." He sat next to Hillary Clinton at Bill Clinton's inaugural address to the nation.

GLS Consulting consisted of four partners and six associates at the time. We offered our services pro bono for six months. We thought our time as consultants would be over. Instead, Aaron asked us to redesign the organization from a hierarchical one to a team-based organization from the bottom up. We trained employees and managers to work in a team-based organization. We evidenced an ROI of $400K. My partner and I co-authored a book chapter about the ROI of training in an ASTD Field book and co-authored another book chapter on top leadership teams. However, the trifecta of a loan too big to sustain, winters too warm for the fleece product, and the cheap imitations of the premier Polartec fabric from China spelled disaster. We provided services for a decade. Unfortunately, the mill could not avoid bankruptcy.

SECRET FIVE:
BE READY FOR CHANGE: IT WILL SHOW YOU THE WAY

We moved on to work in high-tech, first with EMC, and then for several years, we commuted to Washington DC to work with a consulting company's employees who worked with various Federal agencies like the IRS and Coast Guard. Our four partners generated seven-figure revenues throughout the decade.

Then I got the itch to do international work in 2005. With a Blackberry in one hand and portable copy and fax machines, I didn't see the need to spend $250.000 in overhead for offices and a secretary. I cared for my partners and enjoyed my corner office. However, I felt the tectonic plates of technology and business models shifting. I hated leaving my corner office, yet again, but my voice was firm within me. I took my purple ergonomic office chair and books and left our firm on friendly terms. Now I see the pattern of me emerging. I have a ten-year growth spurt. Or has the world changed dramatically since 9-11?

I developed a new business model for my next entrepreneurial venture, Collaborative Networks International. My goals were to work smarter, eliminate overhead, and increase profit. I experienced great relief. No more worrying about providing work for six associates and three other partners. While working from home, however, I missed the camaraderie of my colleagues. However, I liked making more money and working less even more.

Boston had grown into a hotbed of tech entrepreneurialism. During this time, I became an early co-founder of an HVAC company, getting equity in the company instead of having them pay for my coaching and facilitation services. I loved being the founder and President of Collaborative Networks. I substituted collaborating and contracting with other entrepreneurs rather than building a payroll.

Thirty years had flown by. In 2014 we were on the move again. We had a lovely retirement party with the congregation and said our goodbyes. This time I left my home corner office to relocate to Northern New Jersey. We loved Boston, the community, and JP Licks, the best ice cream ever. However, we loved even more for the first time in four decades to live close enough to three of our married children and 14 grandchildren, to actively participate in their daily lives.

SECRET SIX:
PRACTICE AN ADAPTIVE MINDSET

I quickly discovered I loved being a Savta (grandma). However, life had other intentions. I did a favor for a colleague, consulting pro bono with a nonprofit Director for several hours. This led to projects and collaborations that continue to the present day, a decade later. Business pulled me in again albeit at a slower pace. Part of me may have wanted to retire, but the entrepreneur, not so much. My husband happily supported my new business.

I crossed things off my bucket list. I learned to swim, and I taught coaching in a graduate school leadership program. My writing picked up again during the pandemic. I co-authored in 2021 the book *Conversation Secrets for Tomorrow's Leaders*. Two more co-authored books came out in 2023 and 2024 on *Cracking the Rich Code* with Jim Britt.

SECRET SEVEN:
BUILD YOUR ADAPTABILITY MUSCLE-PRACTICE HOPE, MENTAL FLEXIBILITY, CONTINUOUS LEARNING, AND ADAPTING FOR A SUCCESSFUL WORK/LIFE

Woven throughout my history is the courage to find my voice and get it heard to create an impact. Daring to claim my voice and act on it in a way that propels me forward, rather than running in place, is my warrior's journey. The undercurrent of uncertainty, fear, and unpredictability is epigenetically present in a child of survivors and doesn't disappear. Yet, I chose to use it to make me stronger. My brother, the orthopedic surgeon, heals bones; I heal souls. This is our legacy and antidote to hate. We generate ongoing hope in a constantly changing world.

I finally understand my passion for change and why I am such an early-stage adopter of ideas and tech. Twenty years after I began writing and researching work/life dilemmas, I know that work/life balance, harmony, and integration are static and unachievable myths of a bygone era.

Writing this chapter clarifies that work/life balance can be replaced with work/life adaptability. Adaptability appears in most of the top ten leadership skills for success. Learning, unlearning, mental flexibility, hope, and resilience are components of adaptability that we are now learning to measure. Adaptability or an adaptive work/life as I coin this phrase, provides a north star for navigating the accelerated pace of change. May these seven Adaptive Secrets inspire you to embrace an adaptive work/life as you take your next leap forward.

ABOUT DR. MINDY GEWIRTZ

Dr. Mindy Gewirtz

Dr. Mindy Gewirtz, MCC, is the founder and president of Collaborative Networks International, a firm specializing in leadership and executive coaching. The best-selling author of five books, speaker, and entrepreneur, Dr. Mindy collaborates with leaders to enhance their leadership skills and behaviors, preparing them for future success and advancement. Her global clientele spans healthcare, high-tech, biotech, alternative energy, manufacturing, government, and nonprofit sectors. A Master Certified Coach (MCC), Mindy is accredited by the International Coach Federation (ICF) and the European Mentoring and Coaching Council (EMCC Global). She earned her Ph.D. at Boston University and served as Adjunct Faculty at Lewis University, where she taught Coaching Methodology and Coaching/Mentoring courses in the Master of Organizational Leadership (MAOL) program. Additionally, Mindy has mentored numerous coaches from the US, India, Saudi Arabia, and Germany towards their MCC accreditation. Also, a Board-Certified Diplomate (BCD) and licensed psychotherapist in Boston, she has held an adjunct faculty position at Boston University. Mindy is a co-author of "Conversation Secrets for Tomorrow's Leaders: 21 Obvious Secrets Leaders Do Not Use Enough," published in 2021. In the 2023 volume of "Cracking the Rich Code," co-authored with Jim Britt and Kevin Harrington, her chapter focuses on work-life adaptability. She has contributed five book chapters on leadership, teaming, and change management. Mindy and her husband look forward to celebrating their upcoming major anniversary with a tandem skydiving adventure.

Website: https://www.collaborativenetworks.net
Facebook: https://www.facebook.com/collaborativenetworks
LinkedIn: https://linkedin.com/in/collaborativenetworks
Instagram: https://www.instagram.com/mgewirtz1/
Email: mgewirtz@collaborativenetworks.net

CHAPTER 8

Liz Hatcher

STEPPING INTO THE POSSIBLE

As a child, I loved playing make-believe. I would create whole imaginary worlds for myself and my friends, and we would have epic adventures. I lived in the country - the tiny town of Miami in rural New Mexico, to be precise. The town had dirt roads, lots of fields, and lots of irrigation ditches for the ranchers and farmers. My friends and I would spend days on end wandering through those fields and ditches, exploring and imagining; being anything we wanted to be, and shaping our adventure however we wanted it to go.

This imaginative spirit and belief that I can be anything I want and do anything I set my mind to has stuck with me since those early childhood days. Discovering who I wanted to be and what I wanted to do, on the other hand, has been its own adventure.

Growing up, I wanted to be many things - an astronaut, an actress, a singer, a lawyer, an architect, the list goes on! In college, world politics fascinated me, and I had this grand vision of becoming a foreign diplomat. I even spent time working in government as an intern, traveling abroad in Europe and Japan, and studying Russian because I thought I wanted to work for the US Embassy in Moscow. But a funny thing happened when I graduated: I discovered I didn't want any of it. This grand vision I had for myself was going to lead to a life I realized I didn't want.

Now what? I had no idea what was going to come next, what I was going to do, or what I even wanted to do. Who was I? I had no clue.

The next shiny object (because that's really what it was at the time) was the idea of getting into public relations. I honestly can't recall why, but the idea must have sounded cool to 22-year-old me because I was absolutely determined to get a job in PR. This determination led to landing a job with the Portland Rose Festival Association - after hounding the PR Director for months to give me a shot!

I didn't know it at the time, but that job with the Rose Festival set the stage for everything else in my career that has followed. I had an incredibly supportive yet hands-off boss who was happy to just let me run with things. She entrusted me with massive projects and gave me the freedom to get them done as I saw fit. I got to experience first-hand what goes into running a large civic event like the annual, city-wide Rose Festival. Until you are on the inside, it is hard to fully grasp the sheer scope of it. I have a penchant for dreaming big, and I blame the Portland Rose Festival for that.

I came away from that first job full of confidence and belief in who I was. Or so I thought. In hindsight, I was nowhere near figuring myself out. And that confidence... well, let's just say I had some lessons to learn that would shake me to my core. I have proven to myself time and again that I can and should reach beyond my comfort zone, as I have been given the freedom in my jobs and the companies I've worked for to stretch. But I have also been caught off guard by the true motives behind the so-called support of others. It has been in these moments when I have questioned everything about myself.

For example, a few years and a couple of jobs after the Rose Festival, I was hired as the Marketing Director for an international medical device manufacturer. I found out after I was hired that I was the replacement for the VP they intended to fire after I was fully up to speed. He knew it when he interviewed me - everyone knew it - and he did what he could to set me up for failure. I was left in the dark until his final week. Finally, the underlying animosity I had been feeling in the office made sense. But I was still blind to what was really going on, and the undercutting culture continued.

I held my own, but I began to doubt myself. I kept waiting for someone to figure out that I didn't know what I was doing or that I didn't belong. These were the lies I was telling myself. It didn't matter that I was "killing it" in my job, I felt I had to constantly prove myself. Flash forward a few years to the point when the CEO propositioned me, and all those doubts nearly crushed me. In a single moment, I questioned everything about why I had been hired or whether any of my success and accolades on the job were merited. What had I done to bring this on? I was afraid to tell my husband. I was embarrassed to tell anyone. All of my accomplishments and success in the job suddenly felt meaningless.

In hindsight, I know I had no logical reason to doubt myself, but it took time to get over the experience. Part of the healing came with the next job at an ad agency, where I had the same freedom and creativity in my job that I had experienced working at the Rose Festival. But this was even better. I got to work directly with clients and help them solve problems, drive their marketing, and grow their businesses. It was incredibly rewarding, and through it, I discovered another piece of me: serving others can be pure joy!

I left the agency so I could fully embrace being a mom to my son. I was lucky enough to be able to do this. I cherish every minute of those early years, taking my son to school, volunteering in the classroom, exploring parks, discovering new things, and having grand adventures like I did as a little girl. I cried the day I said yes to another job - by then, my son was in middle school. I knew it was the end of a magical chapter, but I also knew it was time. I wasn't sure what I was looking for, but I knew I needed to step back into work to figure it out. There was more I wanted to do; I just didn't know what it was yet.

I'd love to say the next job was a great experience, that it unlocked new opportunities, or that it gave me the boost I needed. It was the exact opposite. It was another blindside - and it tore me apart. It was a small, woman-owned company with an all-female staff. I was in awe of the talent and inspired by the CEO. But what I thought would be a supportive environment was, in reality, a toxic nightmare of manipulation and verbal and emotional abuse. Again, I had the freedom to do my job and found the work itself to be incredibly rewarding, but I was so beaten up by the end that I lost all of my self-confidence. When I finally resigned, I was a shell of what I had been. That empty feeling sounds so foreign to me now, but at the time, it was my truth.

It took me years to undo the damage I caused myself by defining myself by how others treated me. This in itself was self-sabotage. I can blame others all I want for their bad behavior, but I have only myself to blame for how I internalized it. I'm not beating myself up here, just pointing out a lesson I had to learn: who I am has nothing to do with other people. Who I am is defined by me and me alone. Who I want to become is also entirely up to me. At the time, however, I still didn't know who that was.

I don't think I ever stopped believing I could be or do whatever I wanted, though that belief has certainly been challenged. But I did get a little lost along the way to now. With the support of an incredible mentor and a strong community of women, I have learned to accept myself for who I am and to step fully into my own possibility. I have finally discovered that who I want to be is me in this moment. The me who is always looking forward, who will continue to evolve, and who will never stop becoming.

My grandmother told me that the day we stop learning is the day we start dying. I see becoming the same way. We never stop becoming. Life will continue to challenge us, shape us, guide us, and present us with new experiences. As we move through every stage, we continue to grow.

When the idea to start my own business finally emerged, I was working in arguably the best job I'd ever had, with the best boss and the best team. I loved everything about this job and the people and community I served. My job was working for a local chamber of commerce, and it was the precursor to what I am doing now. When I said yes to the position with the chamber, it was not what I thought my next step was going to be. In fact, it was a hard turn in another new direction. It was a gut-check moment, though, and I knew on some level I needed to say yes.

I am so glad I said yes to that job. I regained my confidence, rediscovered the things I love to do most, and found new skills I never thought I would have. I was encouraged and supported to push my own boundaries, and I was allowed to fail. This is probably the most important lesson. It is ok to fail. That's how we learn. That's how we grow. My boss and my team made it a safe place to be vulnerable and to be strong. To fail and to succeed. We cheered each other on, we held each other through tears, and we supported each other through everything the job had in store for us every day.

Yet, I wasn't happy. My poor boss had to sit through many sob sessions in her office while we tried to figure out what my problem was. I say that a bit tongue in cheek. The only problem was that it was time for me to move on and step into my own possibilities. It just took an epiphany one day and a series of unexpected conversations that led to the immediate realization that it was time to go. It was time for me to do my own thing. Once that "pandora's box" was opened, there was no looking back. I quit my job - after giving a nice long notice, so no one was left in the lurch - and stepped out on my own.

Launching and growing my marketing company was an exciting time for me. I had a clear vision of what I wanted to do and the types of clients I wanted to serve, and I had an incredible network of referral partners and other professionals to collaborate with. I was tapping into the things I knew I was good at - branding, content strategy, copywriting - and I was living life fully on my terms.

Happy ending? Not yet. There were still a few lessons to be learned.

While I also like to dream big, I also like saying yes. I'm a people-pleaser, and I hate to let go of a good thing. So, naturally, I joined the chamber I had just left and stepped up to chair the women's networking program I had helped grow while I was on the staff. Never mind that I was launching my business - I figured I could handle both. And for a time, I did.

At the same time, I understood how vital networking was to my success as a business owner. Not only for referrals and clients but also for personal growth. I did not know the first thing about running a business other than how to market and how to do my books. I wanted to talk to other women entrepreneurs, learn from each other, support each other, and share in our journey as business owners. I found that comradery in the networking group I was chairing, and I became fiercely passionate and protective of the group. It was special, and it was rare. I had not found that same culture in any other group I participated in or event I attended.

Despite the program's success, the chamber abruptly shut down the group when it was deemed unnecessary and irrelevant. Once again, I felt blindsided. I was devastated and full of anger and hurt when it happened. I didn't understand why it mattered so much to me (I do now), but I couldn't let it go. Neither could my fellow committee members or the sponsor, all of whom urged me to just start something.

I didn't see what they saw in me, and I didn't understand why I had to be the one to start this new thing. But I did it anyway. I just couldn't let it go.

A year and a half later, as my marketing business was thriving, I found myself still volunteering as the leader of this group. It had grown, and the requests for me to do more for the group were growing. I was reaching a breaking point and becoming resentful of the whole thing. I had a serious attitude of "why me" and really didn't want to do it anymore. But I still couldn't let it go. So I hired a coach.

Wow. Another blindside, but this one was good. I hired the coach, a woman I had met through the group, to help me get better at running my business so I could increase my revenue. What I got was infinitely more valuable. She got me to look at my life, not just my business, in a whole new way. Through her, I was able to remove all the business thoughts cluttering my mind and look at things with my heart. My success was not going to come from doing what I was good at. My success was only going to come by doing what I loved and by doing it with the people I wanted to spend my time with. (You can replace "success" with "happiness" in that last sentence, the point is the same.)

Working with her, this thing I couldn't let go of, that I felt was dragging me down, rose to the top. It was the thing I was supposed to be doing. It was and is my purpose. Talk about energizing! The way forward was so clear! The next thing I did was make a commitment to myself and to this new company - The Women to Women Network (although the name did not come about for a few months). I couldn't volunteer anymore. This wasn't a side gig or a fun project. It was a business, and it deserved my full attention. I knew that by saying yes, I was in it for at least ten years because it would need time to grow, to evolve, to become. I may not have known the full breadth of what would be possible, but I knew it was big. I knew it would be demanding, and I knew it would be worth it.

What I didn't know was how much I would grow in the process. I have had to step out of my comfort zone so many times I no longer know where the boundaries are. I have said yes to so many things I may have forgotten how to say no. This is something my team reminds me to learn and relearn! It is so easy to take on "just one more thing," but I know now that by doing so, I am depriving others of contributing to my vision. And although I surrounded myself with an amazing community of incredible and supportive women who believed in the vision and believed in me, I still had doubts. I still felt like I wasn't up to the task, that I wasn't the leader everyone thought I was.

It took another coach who delivered one final blindside. We had been working on scaling and revenue models when he sent me an urgent message out of the blue. "We have an unfinished conversation. How soon can you talk?" I respected him and figured it must be important. Well, that's an understatement, because what he told me when we chatted changed everything. He told me to stop doubting what I was doing, and to stop worrying about what other people, other leaders, or other organizations were doing. He told me to start leaning in, be the leader I am and step into my own possibility.

In that moment, something clicked, and for the first time, I saw myself as a leader. I finally embraced who I wanted to be - who I knew I could be.

As we expand the company nationally - into yet another uncharted chapter - I realize that I am still becoming. That will never stop, just as I will never stop stepping into the possible. I may not know how to do all the things that need to be done to run this company that has surpassed all of my original ideas, but I do know that I am more than capable of figuring it out. I haven't yet found the end of my possible. I don't think I ever will.

In some way, I am still that little girl running through the fields, having epic adventures with her friends. There really is no better way to describe how I feel about what I do. It is an adventure, I am in control of my story, and it is more fun than I ever could have imagined.

My advice to anyone wondering what they should do next, holding back on their dreams, or waiting until they are ready, have enough experience, skills, knowledge - the list goes on - is to start stepping into your own possible. You are more capable than you think, and what you don't know, you will learn. Mistakes are inevitable, but so is your growth. So trust yourself. Surround yourself with people who share in your vision and who push you to do more. Push yourself. You've got this, and the adventure waiting for you once you start chasing down those dreams - which will only get bigger as you go - will be worth it.

ABOUT LIZ HATCHER

Liz Hatcher

Founder and CEO of Women to Women Network, Liz Hatcher describes herself as an accidental leader. Leadership is something she fell into and then embraced when she realized how she could help others step into their own potential, which is a big part of the backstory behind her rapidly growing organization. Liz is an entrepreneur and creative at heart with a diverse background in marketing, association management, and event production across multiple industries and business settings, from small boutique firms to international corporations.

She believes there is opportunity everywhere you look and in everything you do and says that "it just takes a little creative thinking." This is something she excels at. She gets a thrill from discovering opportunities that help others move forward and enjoys finding new ways to take full advantage of the resources around us.

Website: https://www.wtownetwork.com/
Facebook: https://www.facebook.com/WomentoWomenNetwork
LinkedIn: https://www.linkedin.com/in/lizhatcher427
Instagram: https://www.instagram.com/wtownetwork/

Allison Keeley

THE CIRCUS, DEFINING NORMAL, AND CHOOSING YES!

"How'd you like to work for the circus?"

The slightly sweet smell of hay, dust and elephants hung in the air of the elephant yard on that autumn California morning. It all felt slightly surreal as I tried to absorb the words my graduate professor had just uttered… surely, I had misheard. But no, here we were, a month into my graduate program studying elephant reproduction, and that's exactly what he said.

I stood there, slightly dumbfounded, my mouth gaping like a fish out of water. He smiled an amused yet sympathetic smile and followed with, "They'll fly you out for an interview."

I obviously had many more questions, all of which he answered, and decided it never hurts to interview - I could always decline if it didn't fit.

Long story short… I said yes! After all, how many people get to say, "I ran away with the circus?"
Telling my family was something else. My mom's response was priceless…

"Can I come?"

As you can see, I come by my love of adventure naturally.

And that is really the heart of the journey that led me to where I am today - a love of adventure, saying yes to unusual opportunities without a specific plan, a curiosity for what is possible, and the communication skills to navigate the situations I found myself in after I said "yes."

And the realization that my normal was abnormal.

Let me back up.

My mom has always been the shining example of saying yes to exploring the unknown, which led to my dad accepting a job transfer to Belgium when I was 6 years old - neither of them knew the language. Agreeing to live in a foreign country where you don't know the customs or the language, and you don't have any friends… that's a huge leap of faith! But it was an adventure. It was "we'll figure it out." It'll be a great experience - how often do you get this opportunity?

My mom is also the role model for communication and learning, as well as the unwavering cheerleader for pursuing dreams and trying new things. She's my moving buddy when I pull up stakes and take a job on the other side of the country. I know I can do anything because she always has my back.

My journey has taken me all over the country, through varying paths and industries, but at every stop along the way I have collected communication tools and insights.

I learned to say "yes" to adventure and opportunities as they showed up along the path. And for each "yes," I acquired communication skills which allowed me to succeed in that endeavor and in subsequent "yeses." The communication skills I built for my "yesses" to be successful are what built my business today. Now I take all the skills, tools, insights, and perspectives I acquired along the journey and share them with others so they can succeed in their journeys.

Running away with the circus was like moving to a foreign country all over again. I got little guidance or direction and had to learn the culture, identify key players and how they preferred to operate, figure out how to communicate with people when we didn't speak the same language, and navigate the daily dynamics in a way that acknowledged other's preferences while holding the boundaries that let me do my job well.

And I loved it!

While the decision to leave the circus was a difficult one - especially since they offered me the job full time - I had a master's degree waiting for me to complete, and it seemed foolish to let that opportunity go.

I completed my degree and continued working with animals for many more years, just not while traveling with the circus - although I did go back briefly, and still have many friends from that period in my life.

My path switched from animals to people after a bucket-list safari in Tanzania.

At the time, I was working at a zoo taking care of a variety of animals, including lions and tigers. Going on that safari was life changing for me. It really highlighted how much I was still passionate about the animals - and I always would be. But it also held up the mirror showing me I was no longer happy doing what I did as a zookeeper, and really hadn't been for years.

This revelation caused me to start exploring what I could do differently. When I got back, I decided to apply for an animal manager job at the zoo. It would still be working in the zoo, allowing me to stay connected to the animals, but with more of an emphasis on people. I like people - I always have.

Well, the zoo had different ideas. One of my coworkers accused me of doing something I hadn't done. And management, instead of talking with me about the situation or verifying whether or not I had done the thing that I was accused of, instead unilaterally decided to move me from my primary area of focus and responsibility to an entirely different area - with absolutely no warning. And they somehow thought it wouldn't be seen as a disciplinary action!

I was taken completely aback! I said, "If you think the rest of the animal keepers aren't going to recognize that you taking me off my primary string and making me work a different string isn't disciplinary, you are delusional."

And shockingly, when I worked on the other string, none of the things which I was being accused of happened - because they didn't happen on my primary string either!

After working the other string for a couple of weeks, I reflected on my situation. I realized this was the Universe's way of making sure that the message is crystal clear: This is no longer where you are supposed to be! I said to myself: "You know what? I don't know what I'm going to do next, but I'm not doing this anymore! It's not worth it. It doesn't bring me joy or satisfaction, and it doesn't fill my heart or spirit… I'm out!"

So, I walked in Monday morning, and I gave my notice.

I don't think I've ever seen a manager quite so stunned in my life! I probably could have knocked her over with a feather!

Certainly not the outcome they were expecting when they took the disciplinary action that "wasn't disciplinary."

Then I told my fellow keepers I was leaving. Their responses were along the lines of: "So, what are you going to do next? Where are you going? What job do you have lined up?"

To which I replied: "I don't have a job and I have no idea what I'm doing next."

They were dumbfounded! "How could you possibly be leaving what you're doing without knowing what you're doing next?"

It had never occurred to them that that was possible.

But hey, that's what I'm going to do. Because if I stay in this mess that makes me crazy and sucks my soul dry, I'm not going to figure out the next step. I won't be able to see it, and I won't be able to say "yes" when possibility pops up in the middle of my path.

I quit.

I then spent a year in personal growth and development.

It was part way through that journey that someone pointed out to me that my ongoing love of learning, and teaching what I've learned to somebody else, combined with my natural cheerleading tendencies (thank you Mom) are the characteristics that make a good coach.

That is how I ended up starting my first business as a coach.

It was my first foray, my first exposure really, to entrepreneurship; because it was so NOT a part of my upbringing! My father is the 'same career for 40 years until I retire' guy.

Which led me to the next challenge: how do you start your own business?

This was very foreign to me.

And I gave it my best shot!

I brought together my natural communication skills with my willingness to "leap without a Plan B" and sought to help my clients do the same.

I loved working with clients and helping them see things differently. I was easily able to identify the point where they couldn't see what wasn't working for themselves and shine a bright light on it. Then I would help them navigate to the outcome on the other side.

But I didn't know how to run the business. I didn't know how to market and finding new clients was painfully hard. There were so many little details that running a business requires that I didn't know how to do. And with no support network, I found myself sitting at home alone with no one to talk to and no idea how to change it.

As a very extroverted person who likes lots of human contact, I was starving for human interaction. So, I gave up trying to be a solopreneur and I got a job at a veterinary hospital.

I got to work with animals - this time it was dogs and cats, not lions and tigers and bears and monkeys - but I got the animal contact and I got to spend time with people. I handled customer service, which is where I started my working life, answering phones. I'm really good at hearing what needs to be solved, rather than what someone says they think needs to be solved.

I was there for a while and got to sample all the positions in the clinic. In fact, by the time I left I had done every role except veterinarian (because of the education and licensing they are required to have). I love to learn, so give me something new to learn and I'll go do it really well for you.

Again, eventually I hit the point where I realized, "Nope - this isn't where I need to be. I keep banging my head against a wall that's never going to change. There is no door here - it's time to make my own door."

I struggled with wanting to stay, and fix or modify what wasn't working, versus needing to find the right fit for me and being willing to say goodbye when it was best for me. When constant stress starts to weaken my immune system and affect my appetite, it's a sign that I'm in the wrong place.

I once again said to myself, "This is no longer working for me. It is sucking my soul and making me sick. I'm done."

I walked away.

"What are you doing next?"

"I have no idea. Don't care. Doesn't matter. Bye!"

It turns out walking away from what isn't working before having the next step lined up isn't normal…but that has turned out to be my path.

I took some time off and then found something else to do part time. It was a new industry and a new adventure, and I learned other new skills and met new people… but it still wasn't the thing.

Then a friend said to me "You are an amazing coach, and the world needs what you have to offer. Let's figure out who you want to coach. What kind of coaching do you want to do?"

What a great question! It got me thinking…

I remembered somebody that I had worked with before. I was on a road trip. My fellow passengers were a mother and grown son. An hour into our eight-hour drive, the two of them started having a conversation that they had clearly had many times before to no avail, with no resolution, which left everybody in a miserable space. I disrupted their long-standing pattern and started coaching them. I coached them for seven hours, while driving, and at the end of those seven hours we had figured out what was not working, where the miscommunication was happening, and found a new solution. They negotiated a new set of expectations, and that conversation was finally brought to a close, never to be repeated again.

I spent the entire trip helping them clarify their issues and work through them. Was I exhausted? Not a bit. Instead of feeling like I needed to sleep for twelve hours straight, I stepped out of that car ready for round two.

That was my signal that communication coaching is where I shine.

Then I looked at other coaching I had done and saw other instances that were similar.

I had a couple I had been working with over the course of a few months. We had all been in a workshop together and I would be leaving at 6 a.m. the next morning. They asked for one more session before I left, because there was one more big conversation they needed to have and wanted some support with. So, after all the workshop farewells and drawn-out goodbyes with the rest of the group, we started coaching around 10 o'clock at night and didn't wrap up until 2 o'clock the next morning.

Part way through we hit a roadblock: I could see the woman visibly swallow her words - her brain was filtering and editing what comes out of her mouth because she didn't want to hurt her partner.

I had an idea.

I had recently learned a technique called automatic writing, where writing without stopping or editing can lead to better access to subconscious thoughts, because the act of writing stimulates different areas of our brain and helps us let go of logic.

My client has (sign) language in her hands.

My brain and my intuition put the two pieces together and came up with an experiment: taking two seemingly unrelated skills and combining them. Could sign language access the right-brain the way automatic writing did to override left-brain logic? I had no idea ahead of time if it would work, but it didn't hurt to try it.

So, I asked the couple to trust me and try something a bit off-the-wall.

"Hey, tell me what's going on with your hands - in sign language. With a very large caveat that you need to translate with your mouth because I don't speak sign language."

It worked beautifully! As soon as she started talking with her hands, all of what she needed to say came out of her mouth! Then it was out in the open and we could work through it. They had a hard conversation from a place of partnership and found their solution to move forward.

Yeah, that's the stuff! That's what I love to provide for people!

Again, I wasn't tired and dragging, I was energized. I had taken a skill we had just learned and a skill one person in the relationship had and blended the two to create an outcome that might not have been possible otherwise.

So now I knew I wanted to help people have more effective communication, allowing them to navigate difficult or uncomfortable conversations with more ease.

This time around when I started my business, I knew I needed a support network. My friend who nudged me back into coaching connected me with a network of women entrepreneurs who were about supporting each other. They helped me learn what I didn't know (and didn't know I didn't know), shared resources which worked for them, and connected me to other women who could help me. They helped me celebrate my wins and supported me in the inevitable low moments where all I wanted to do was give up.

I found my own coaches to keep me moving forward, taking through obstacles, creating goals and deadlines for myself and keeping me accountable. I learned that coaching comes in many forms and flavors, and that finding the right fit of personality and style matters. Some only ask questions designed to help you find the answers yourself. Others give you checklists and formulas that create a roadmap for you to go do on your own. And some act like mentors, sharing their knowledge and adding to your toolbox, as well as asking questions to make you think, challenging you and cheering you on as you go.

The mentor, or sports coach, style is both the coach I like to work with and my own coaching style. I now take all those skills and tools, experiences, and insights that I have been acquiring for decades, and I apply them to my human communication coaching. I help my clients see the places they can't see for themselves, get the tools that they were never taught - because we don't teach this kind of stuff in school - and help them build relationships, both personally and professionally, that are more effective and connected. They are supported and can pursue their goals and grow as human beings.

So, for anyone thinking of building their own business, consider these things:

Figure out what your 'SPARK' is! That thing that causes you to say, "Ohh, that lit me up like a fire! More please!" Find what gives you that spark and then follow that.

Find a good support network. One that can help you learn what you don't know and connect you with resources. One that will support you as you navigate the hard moments as well as celebrate with you when something goes right. Because BOTH are important.

Get a coach. Figure out what is a good fit for your personality, needs and style and make the investment. There may be some trial and error, you may decide you need more than one for different areas. It can feel scary and daunting, but it's worth it!

And remember…it's not linear, there will always be ups and downs, good days and bad, but you can do it.

ABOUT ALLISON KEELEY

Allison Keeley

Allison Keeley is an interpersonal communication coach and trainer, veteran public speaker, and Owner of Lioness Communication. Her work equips people with the tools and perspectives to have clear, proactive communication as well as effectively navigate difficult conversations, especially in the workplace.

Allison began coaching as a Peer Counselor in school and now blends her unique background of 20+ years working with animals with her degree in Social-Psycho Linguistics to help her clients understand and dissolve their communication blocks. She combines insights from the animal kingdom with her own knowledge, skills, and intuition, to help people bridge the gaps created by the communication misses that are often a result of our animal instincts.

When she's not helping clients from around the world, she enjoys spending time outdoors with her family and dog near Portland, OR, as well as traveling and exploring the world, or curled up with a good book.

Website: https://lionesscommunication.com/
Facebook: https://www.facebook.com/LionessCommunicationCoaching
LinkedIn: https://www.linkedin.com/in/allisonkeeley1/
Instagram: https://www.instagram.com/lionesscommunicationcoaching/

CHAPTER 10

Dawn Renee

THE DIARY OF A DIVA: UNBREAKABLE SPIRIT

As a single hard-working mother with an entrepreneurial side hustle, I wear many hats: daughter, mama, friend, dog lover, entrepreneur, nature enthusiast, model, photographer, and now, proudly, an inspirational speaker. My purpose on the planet is to empower myself and others to rise above life's storms - just as I have had to do. But getting to where I am now wasn't a walk in the park. Like many of us, my journey was paved with setbacks lurking around every corner. By age 17, I'd experienced more hardship than most people see in a lifetime. From being in foster care, experiencing domestic violence, losing a pregnancy, having a brother in and out of juvenile detention, being subjected to verbal, mental, and physical abuse (and later escaping) - even homelessness - I have overcome these and other experiences and come out with my spirit intact.

Imagine standing at the base of a colossal mountain, its peaks veiled in swirling mist, beckoning you to ascend its daunting heights. This was my reality one spring when I decided to confront Mount St. Helens - a test of courage, resilience, and personal transformation. Little did I know that this journey would mirror the struggles of my own life and illuminate the profound lessons I would learn along the way.

The adventure began with boundless excitement. The crisp air was invigorating, the scenery mesmerizing. But as I progressed, the mountain grew steeper, and the thin air felt like it was compressing my chest. Doubts began to seep in. Each step was a battle against the terrain, my body, and my mind. The summit seemed a world away. I was overwhelmed by the enormity of the challenge, feeling tiny and insignificant against nature's vastness.

This journey was not just a physical ascent, but a metaphor for the mountains we all face in life. Each challenge we encounter can feel as insurmountable as a mountain peak shrouded in mist. It is through confronting these challenges - whether they be personal, emotional, or professional - that we discover our true strength and resilience.

For almost ten weeks, every Sunday at 7:00 a.m., I met an incredible group of women at the local transit center, and together, we traveled to our weekly hiking destinations. The trails became progressively more intense and challenging, but I kept showing up. I didn't always make it to the top. Sometimes, I ended up with injuries or found myself crying along the way. But each time, I was comforted and reminded that the mountain would always be there. I reminded myself that I showed up for me, that I did the things that mattered.

Each hike was a testament to the strength and resilience within me. I felt stronger, not just physically but mentally. Surrounded by women from diverse backgrounds, I was inspired to grow and become the woman I never thought I could be. I shared my stories, and week after week, women would reach out, telling me how I inspired them or how their stories resonated with mine. I didn't realize the impact I was having. I was helping others step out of their comfort zones, create new possibilities, and embrace their inner divas.

Growing up, I was always the husky girl - never athletic. As I transitioned into roles of motherhood and survival, my life seemed perpetually filled with trials and tribulations. From my tumultuous relationship with my mother to the complexities of my personal relationships, it felt like nothing I did was ever good enough. Why should I choose to do something for myself when there were more pressing responsibilities?

When I started hiking, what was meant to be relaxing became internally unpleasant. Feelings of failure surfaced when I didn't meet my goals. Instead of celebrating my accomplishments, I felt defeated. I knew this mindset had to change. I began to rethink and start my days differently, using words of affirmation. I transformed the voice in my head to say, "This diva can do anything. This diva can climb mountains."

I continued to share my journey on social media, documenting both my triumphs and defeats. The mountain would always be there, ready for my next adventure. Comparing hiking a mountain to life's challenges, I realized that I couldn't give up on life, just as I wouldn't give up on climbing a mountain. Each week, we showed up to new locations, embracing new adventures. The excitement of the unknown was thrilling. Sometimes that voice in my head would creep in, telling me I couldn't do it. My body wouldn't always allow me to finish a hike, and I'd feel crushed. But I learned to thank my body for taking me on these adventures. Instead of focusing on the negative, I cherished the positives and congratulated myself for showing up.

There was a time when I didn't have time to hike - or at least, that's what I told myself. But I realized that we all have things that make us happy. I hadn't known this until I allowed myself to experience these things. I started making time for myself, whether it was hiking, kayaking, or simply showing up for myself. I began doing things, saying yes to myself - the diva way.

Each challenge was a mountain - seemingly insurmountable, yet each one taught me resilience and strength. Escaping an abusive relationship, I emerged from this and other battles with my spirit intact, ready to conquer whatever came next. Just like climbing Mount St. Helens, every step forward demanded courage and determination.

A significant part of my early life was marked by a strained relationship with my mother and her struggle with mental illness. Yet, years later as I got older, I could see a flicker of love beneath the tumultuous surface. Understanding her struggles and stories was a labyrinthine process. Both of my parents passed away in 2019, just before COVID-19. While I am relieved that they didn't have to endure the trials of lockdown, their absence made the pandemic period even more isolating.

My experiences were not just external hardships but also internal battles. The root cause of my struggles was self-love. I grappled with managing my emotions, relationships, and overall well-being. My inner child - and by extension, my daughter - mirrored my self-doubt. The energy I projected said, "I am not worthy of complete love." This realization was painful - it highlighted the potential impact on my daughter's early years. Words and actions are one thing, but the energy we exude speaks louder, influencing those around us, especially our children.

People-pleasing and past traumas - some conscious and others buried deep - were hurdles I had to overcome. The darkness threatened to consume me, but a flicker of defiance remained. Giving up was never an option. Although moments of depression, anxiety, anger, and shame still occasionally creep in, they no longer hold dominion over me. I have discovered a core strength, an unwavering belief in my inherent goodness - a strength that fuels my persistence to strive for a better version of myself.

Navigating through my career and entrepreneurial journey has been a multifaceted adventure. Each role demands its own set of skills - organization, compassion, multitasking, and resilience. Each obstacle encountered has become a stepping stone toward growth.

The launch of Little Dash of DIVA marked a significant turning point. I decided to infuse everything I do with the DIVA way, which stands for Dedication, Intention, Vision, and Action. This approach has guided every choice and direction I've taken. With Dedication, I commit fully to my goals, no matter how challenging they seem. Intention ensures that I have a clear purpose and focus in all my endeavors. Vision helps me see beyond the immediate obstacles, keeping me motivated towards my long-term aspirations. Action is about taking consistent steps forward, transforming my dreams into reality.

Little Dash of DIVA evolved into networking events that gathered women from all walks of life, fostering connections and building communities. I became a divalicious life guide, crafting tools to help women discover and nurture their inner diva. Witnessing their transformation and glow has been one of the most empowering experiences of my life. I could not have achieved any of this without the unwavering support of my family, friends, and colleagues. I am profoundly blessed.

When I first took the stage to share my personal story, fear and self-doubt overwhelmed me. The thought of exposing my most intimate struggles to a room full of strangers was terrifying. Yet, in that moment of vulnerability, I discovered a profound truth: vulnerability is not a weakness, but a powerful force for personal and collective growth.

Vulnerability feels like standing on the edge of a cliff, gazing into the abyss. It's about laying bare our deepest fears, insecurities, and wounds. This act of openness can be daunting because it strips away our protective layers and reveals our true selves. But it's through this raw honesty that we forge genuine connections with others.

Sharing my story of overcoming adversity was a profound act of vulnerability. It allowed me to connect with others on a deeply personal level, creating a ripple effect of healing and empowerment. Even in the face of immense fear, embracing our true selves can lead to unexpected rewards.

Today, I am more than just a survivor; I am a thriving beacon of empowerment. Whether guiding DIVAS on mountain adventures, embracing the serenity of DIVAS on the Water, pioneering "COME YAK with ME" - a kayaking networking group that fosters community and connection - or connecting women through coffee conversations - my mission remains clear: to create spaces where women can connect, grow, and flourish.

As I stand before you, I hope to ignite a fire in your souls, whispering, "Never give up on your dreams!" With unwavering determination and the support of loved ones, we can overcome any obstacle and rewrite our narratives. Life throws us curveballs, but within each of us lies the power to create a life filled with joy, purpose, and boundless possibility.

So, as you face your own mountains, whether literal or metaphorical, remember that every challenge is an opportunity to discover your inner strength. Embrace the discomfort as part of your growth and find joy in the journey, not just the destination. We are all capable of more than we realize, and the view from the summit is always worth the climb.

Together, let's support each other, celebrate every victory, and continue to rise above life's storms. Dream big, hold onto hope, and never stop believing in yourselves. With the DIVA way as our guide, let's dedicate ourselves to our dreams, set clear intentions, envision our success, and take actionable steps towards our goals. Let's create a community where each woman can shine, grow, and achieve her fullest potential.

Dedication:

For Emily, my daughter - our journey together has been filled with both challenges and triumphs. From navigating the toughest times to celebrating our victories, you have been my constant source of strength and joy. Watching you blossom into the incredible woman you are today is a testament to your resilience and spirit. Your growth and achievements fill me with immense pride, and I am grateful every day for the bond we share. Your ability to face life's hurdles with grace and courage reminds me of the power of love and perseverance.

To Terrence, my son - your presence in my life has been a powerful force of transformation. Your drive and determination have not only pushed me to exceed my own limits but also taught me to love more deeply and genuinely. Your energy and enthusiasm have been a driving force in my personal growth, and your belief in me has been a source of inspiration. The way you face life's challenges head-on and the love you show so freely have profoundly impacted my heart and soul. You have shown me that the capacity to grow and love is boundless, and I cherish every moment we share.

From Apala to Coach - your unwavering support and love have been my anchor through the storms of life. Even during the most chaotic times, you stood by my side, offering encouragement and understanding. Your belief in me, even when I struggled to believe in myself, has been a guiding light. Your kindness and patience have helped me become a better person and have shown me the true meaning of unconditional love.

And to Mom and Dad - you are deeply missed, but your memory lives on in every step I take and every challenge I overcome.

ABOUT DAWN RENEE

Dawn Renee

Dawn Renee' is a dynamic speaker, advocate and now author, on a mission to help everyone live their best life with a Little Dash of Diva! She's all about helping women understand the power of showing up and shining bright. Born and raised in the Pacific NW, Dawn Renee' faced a rollercoaster of challenges early on. But did she let that stop her? Absolutely not! Her personal story is a shining example of resilience and perseverance.

Dawn Renee' recently launched Little Dash of Diva, dedicated to empowering women to reach their full potential. She's all about creating a supportive environment that boosts self-confidence, promotes positive body image, and provides the tools for success with the power of D.I.V.A. Little Dash of Diva's mission? To build a community of strong, independent, and empowered women who make a fabulous impact on the world - while making every day a D.I.V.A. day!

Website: https://littledashofdiva.godaddysites.com
Facebook: https://facebook.com/hey.hey.its.dawn.renee
LinkedIn: https://www.linkedin.com/in/dawn-renee-14a68a37
Instagram: https://www.instagram.com/heyhey_its_dawnrenee

CHAPTER 10

TAKING THE LEAP

CHAPTER 11

Rukshana Triem

LESSONS FROM THE BRINK OF DEATH

The Doctor called and said, "I suggest you alert your family members - I don't think your husband is going to make it. You should start planning for a funeral."

It was one week before Thanksgiving weekend. The weather in the Northwest was starting to get cold, wet and rainy. A friend and I had gone snowshoeing. As we sat down to have our hot chocolate with a shot of fireball (a whiskey that goes well with hot chocolate), the phone rang.

"Shana!!!" A panicked voice came from my brother-in-law….

"Your husband Philip called and is not feeling well - so he called me to let him know that he is having stomach pains - but he's so embarrassed to call me because he knows you're out enjoying the snow and playing with your friends."

I knew I had to return home at once. I had to apologize to my friend, and we snowshoed back to the parking lot and drove an hour back home to take him to the hospital.

After a few tests, they told him that he would have to undergo surgery for a simple blood clot. They expected him to be released from the hospital within 24 hours.

What started as a simple stomach pain rapidly escalated into an intense and traumatic ordeal. He underwent emergency surgery, and over the next 12 days, he endured nine more surgeries.

Within just 24 hours, I found myself thrust into a whirlwind of panic, worry, and uncertainty, making critical decisions about his health. Blood transfusions, an induced coma to give his body a desperately needed break from working so hard - each choice weighed heavily on my heart. The relentless cycle of hope and fear became our new reality, each moment a battle for his survival.

What should have been a simple surgery led into complications that kept him in the hospital for nine months. I got calls in the middle of the night to make decisions for the doctor as he updated me on the potential ramifications - and to help me plan for the worst.

My body cringed and stressed. I couldn't eat. I was tired, bordering on exhausted. I couldn't make decisions - even when my friends were calling to help. I couldn't even tell them what I wanted. I just wanted to take a sleeping pill and go to sleep and stay in denial.

I asked myself, "Is this really happening? Or am I dreaming?"
Amidst these traumatic events, I continued to communicate with my family via group messages to update them. I found days where I was sleeping at the hospital. I spent day after day in the hospital next to him,

watching his vitals praying and visioning the best outcome, while staving off my worst fears of what could happen.

This incident put my husband in the hospital for 90 days. The fact that he survived is nothing short of a miracle! Each day, with countless hours spent visiting and spending the night in the hospital, I watched his heart rate fluctuate and witnessed the necessity of blood transfusions. Sitting on that chair, I was forced to confront the terrifying possibility of losing him. I imagined life without him, and the scenarios that played out in my mind were haunting. The sense of an uncertain future was overwhelming, making every moment in that hospital room a battle against my deepest fears.

My husband had taken care of all the house finances, the mortgage, bills and credit cards. My worst fear started to creep when that fateful call came from the doctor.

My worst nightmare began in started asking friends questions that I never thought I would ask: Will the life insurance pay for the funeral? What was his wish for his burial? (We never talked about that.)

I was angry for not preparing for the worst-case scenario. I hear people talk about how they plan their death just as they plan their living- but I wasn't prepared. And I was really scared.

After digging into files to call the life insurance companies, it was a relief to find the paperwork in organized folders, thanks to my husband's systems. Philip is one of the most organized people I know. When I first met him, he insisted on taking on the bills. Since I am so used to taking care of myself as a single mother and running the household, I soon realized that my organization systems fell far short of his! Like choosing our battles in any relationship, I gave in on that one. Philip took care of the finances, mortgage, real estate investments and other matters required in running our household.

I am no stranger to hard times. In the late 1980's my both parents decided to leave the country of Mozambique. My dad was in the early career of the military and my mom was enjoying her fruits of hard work at a bank - then the war in Mozambique began. They left all their belongings, just taking things that held memories like photo albums and my mom's wedding dress (thinking they would later sell it for money to survive).

We fled the country on foot over mountain ranges, which exposed me to the first experience in the outdoors, leaving my birth country due to the war, only to arrive in a small village. My dad soon found a job driving import and export trucks, while we stayed in a hut.

I remember going to school and studying under the shade of a mango tree, sitting on the dirt to smooth and practice writing English words. I first learned how to write my name this way. This practice is still happening in rural areas where they don't have the necessities for school supplies, or the government is not funding education.

After moving from one city to another in Malawi, my family decided to move to Zambia - yet another country in Africa. Learning the language and adapting to change was hard enough - but what I really struggled with is not having long-term friends. Because of that, I now make sure I create friendships to last.

Living in the refugee camp In Lusaka, Zambia taught me many important lessons. I learned how to wait for food in long lines, feeling the sun peel my skin. Sometimes I had to cut into the line, not knowing that I would be doomed if I didn't make it in enough time for my family to have food.

By taking on this task as early as 12 years of age, I learned to take responsibility for my siblings, cooking for them and caring for their wellbeing while my parents were off looking for small jobs to get us by in the city. My mom was also taking classes on how to speak English because she was the spokesperson for the family. I drew on that strength when I was suddenly faced with my husband's multiple surgeries and recovery.

When it came time to leave, I was grateful that my husband was taken care of by amazing doctors and nurses during his hospitalization. But it was still hard to see him not able to get rest.

After his hospitalization, he even had to find the strength to learn how to walk again. I advocated for him to come home because I knew if he came home, he would heal faster. Getting adequate sleep and rest in our dream home - which we had just bought two years prior - let him recover with a beautiful backdrop of beautiful trees and a creek in the backyard.

Every day I had to face my fears:
What will happen to the house?
Will I lose everything we so worked hard for?
Will I lose my husband too?
But we pushed through day by day, attending doctor appointments, physical therapy, social worker meetings and whatever was required to make a plan for him to keep moving, heal, and get stronger.
When he came home, we both had to learn how to maneuver with his new physical deficits.

My husband says I was a bully when it came to strength training. I couldn't sleep down-stairs, so I insisted he had to learn how to navigate the steps upstairs to our bedroom - even if it took him an hour to get up those seven steps. I knew that if I couldn't sleep, I couldn't take care of him.

He got better. He got stronger and went back to normal, but what came after that is the resentment, the anger, the fear, the uncertainty.

I resented the fact that after I advocated for him, I still had to take care of all the everyday things such as changing his wound, fixing his food, scheduling doctor appointments and the like. I was the nurse, the mental health worker, the physical therapist and the cheerleader. And while that gave him the strength he needed; it left me exhausted.

There were days I wanted to leave and have the hospital take care of him. Was this selfish of me? All I knew was that it boiled down to exhaustion, and in part being in denial that all of this was happening. But after having to care for my siblings earlier in life, I knew that when life happens, you still have to show up and go on because people need you. But I felt stuck.

What I learned in this situation is how to ask for help - probably the hardest thing for me to do. I asked friends to give me respite, go for a walk, go for a hike, ask the kids to come and help and family members. This also led me to become humble and be willing to ask and to sit and receive the help. It was food being dropped off, wine to make me sleep, sleeping pills, walks, or just someone to come over and watch a movie with. It was getting a break from the situation.

I had to address some tough questions during this process:
Could I have prevented his sickness?
What would life have been if he did pass away?
Can I receive the support others are willing to provide - and ask for it?

I decided to share my story in my first book called "Living from Strength & Faith a Rough Hike from Refugee to Success." After writing a book, I created another big goal to start sharing my message not on one stage - but many stages. I started small by joining networking groups, applying for speaking gigs, getting involved in the community, talking and asking the right questions. I started sharing my journey by doing Facebook Lives, then creating courses on YouTube and built the confidence to finally speak on stage.

I realized I did so much in the matter of six years before my husband's illness. I built a business, a community, courses, wrote books, articles for magazines, appeared in many podcast groups, led some amazing women's retreats in all parts of Oregon. I even traveled around the world to share messages of inspiration on big stages.

But who am I? I continue to feel like I am just a little girl from the refugee camp. Looking back, I can see that I have designed the life I have envisioned - a lifestyle I had always dreamed of. This all did not come easily for me. I had to deal with a lot of negative thinking, reflecting and working on myself. This has been a daily battle of overcoming my negative thoughts. Despite my limiting thinking, I have realized that my story and my past is here to help others. I have a message that someone is waiting to hear, and they can only hear it from me.

I am always grateful for my past. I have worked in jobs ranging from preschool teacher to trainer for childcare providers - even at a call center for credit card services. One year, I worked at Target stores during the holiday season to get some money and ahead for Christmas presents for my kids.

It wasn't until I got my B.A. degree in Human Development and then went to work for a nonprofit to be a parent advocate when I realized I had a lot to offer. In fact, I came to realize that I knew so much that I should become a coach. At that time my husband was just getting into his personal development journey, so I went with him through a three-day seminar on goal setting. I then came back to starting my outdoor community that has been very successful and has over 1000 members in each chapter.

This led into hiring a coach to help me build my business. In three years, I worked with three different coaches who helped me build my coaching practice on what it is today Women's Lifestyle Coaching, helping women create their best life through one-on-one coaching. Women's Lifestyle Coaching is a platform and a community of women who step up into the Entrepreneur world and create their best life on their own terms. I am so fortunate to be able to surround myself with women who are able to step on stage for the first time and share their stories, host their first event, go on their first outdoor adventure or create that one thing they have been wanting.

It wasn't until I got three clients that gave me the confidence to give a six-week notice to my employer that I was going to leave. In between then I had saved up six months of living experiences, and I had faith and trust that I was going to do what it took to make this business work.

My business took many turns and shifts - and seven years later I have gained more freedom, time doing the things I love, while also learning a lot about business, relationships and investments. I continue working on myself by meditating, working on my journal and understanding that my limiting thoughts are lies and there to protect me. I know that I am in the right place and the right time.

I have surrounded myself with amazing women in businesses by networking and in masterminds that help me elevate my thinking and be influenced by higher achievers and those who know more than I do.

From all of these adversities in my life, I learned that life goes on, even if there is a pause, a death, a natural catastrophe - life will go on, and people do move on. And as a coach, I have brought these lessons to my clients, whether I am facilitating a retreat, coaching clients one-on-one or speaking on stage. I have learned that life is always ups and down, if we go up, we will go down, when we go down…you know if something terrible has happened there is good coming up next and it's just around the corner.

I was able to bounce back, build strength and have a stronger faith - and after what ended up being a two-year break from my business, I could come back with new excitement, new resolve, and more compassion and life lessons to share with my clients.

Running a successful coaching business and guiding nature retreats has been a wild ride. I have been able to facilitate retreats all over the world, stand before many people sharing my transformation story of being a former refugee, and changing my story of healing journey of sexual abuse.

After putting my business on pause for two years, I learned that life pause is a great reminder that in order to move forward we need to sit still and reflect, journal so that we can create amazing things.

In my pause year while running my business, I had to cancel scheduled retreats across several countries - including presentations on big stages - and turn down some major projects. I am very grateful for this pause, because it gave me the strength to value what was important in my life, not just my career and money. I thought about reaching out to his business partner to sell one of our properties, but we were able to manage to live on our credit cards and savings.

And while I had to turn down some major projects during Philip's illness, I am super grateful for this pause because it gave me the strength to value what was important in my life - not just my career and money. I thought about reaching out to his business partner to sell one of our properties, but we were able to manage to live on our credit cards and our savings to get through this challenging time.

I am grateful for my adversities in my life, facing the trauma of living in the refugee camp, waiting in lines not knowing if I would make it to the beginning of the lines to be able to fetch food for my family. I have learned to shift my story from adversity to triumph. I have learned the lessons and gained the knowledge and wisdom I needed to face the challenge of taking care of my husband. And because of where I came from, I could learn the lessons along the way. The resiliency I developed in my early childhood has positioned me to handle things totally differently so that today I can be humble and have compassion for others. Looking back, I had adversity in my youth as well - but nothing could have fully prepared me to handle this situation with my husband Philip.

My husband Philip is thriving again, living his best life and doing what he loves, supporting and loving his family, playing monopoly in investing properties, climbing mountains with me and exploring lakes. His passion in life is heading up the Firmina Foundation, which helps to educate, empower and provide schooling in rural Africa.

ABOUT RUKSHANA TRIEM

Rukshana Triem

As a former refugee from Mozambique, I transformed my experiences into a mission to support parents and child care providers on their healing journeys. Specializing in life-changing habits, I offer coaching, nature retreats, and practical insights through conferences and webinars.

I'm also the author of Living from Strength & Faith, which tells the story of my journey from refugee to success.

I founded Women's Lifestyle Coaching and the Firmina Foundation, a nonprofit dedicated to expanding quality education in Mozambique. When I'm not working, I volunteer at a women's shelter, lead outdoor adventures, and enjoy time with my husband with our kids and nieces.

Website: http://womenslifestylecoaching.com/
Facebook: https://www.facebook.com/rukshana.hafez
LinkedIn: https://www.linkedin.com/in/rukshana-triem/
Instagram: https://www.instagram.com/rukshana_hafez_triem/

CHAPTER 11

Edith Wolek

FROM SHADOWS TO SPOTLIGHT: EMBRACING PASSION TO TRANSFORM LIVES

Growing up, I often found myself daydreaming about a future where I was a significant figure. I imagined having a beautiful, happy family as well as being known for making a positive impact in the world. This dream was nebulous but persistent, shaping my childhood imaginings. I envisioned myself as a TV presenter, much like Oprah Winfrey, although Oprah was not yet an influential figure at that time. My young mind saw her as an embodiment of what I aspired to be - a powerful, empathetic leader. A voice for women everywhere ready to share their courageous stories with the world. The image of me holding a microphone, engaging with people and being a conduit for their stories was vivid and recurring.

My earliest attempts to bring my dream to life involved a tape recorder, a common gadget of my childhood. I would conduct mock interviews, reporting on mundane topics like the weather, just to practice. However, each time I played back the recordings, I was disheartened by the sound of my voice. The voice I heard didn't match the one I imagined, and this dissonance made me question my dream. I began to doubt whether I was cut out for a career in front of the camera, given my apparent dissatisfaction with such a crucial aspect of it.

A particularly vivid memory from my childhood revolves around Mother's Day performance of Little Red Riding Hood which was organized in my neighbourhood. I was cast as the main character. I remember being on a handmade stage, dancing and hopping around pretending to pick flowers all around me. I was fully immersed in the role. However, something significant happened during the performance that marked a turning point for my self-confidence. At one point, I saw the stage empty, so I decided to come out from behind the curtains and continoue to perform, only to hear someone shouting at me: "It's not your turn!". This public admonishment left a lasting impression on me. My inner child internalized the message that perhaps it would never be my turn to shine, to be on a stage, performing as my authentic self. This incident reinforced my growing belief that I wasn't meant for the stage. Through out the years I was collecting more and more evidence to support this belief which stayed with me until recenly.

Even just a few years ago whilst attending corporate conference, I whispered to a work colleague looking at a speaker on the stage: "I could never be able to do that! I would die if they were to ask me to speak on the stage." I was convinced that being a confident speaker was way beyond my capabilities. Even more so as English is my second language.

During my childhood, there were few specific situations that played a significant role in shaping my early self-doubt, fear, anxiety and worry. My upbringing was marked by a lack of emotional support. Frequent shouting and arguing left me feeling scared, uncertain, unworthy and feeling not good enough. Any sport or accademic accomplishments I achieved were swept under the rug and not seen as anything significant.

In my early elementary school years, I've taken part in intense swimming lessons as I was a very passionate swimmer. I was chosen to take part in swimming competitions between schools which resulted in my proudest moment by far. At the age of 14 I achieved two medals, silver and bronze. I hoped the next step for me was to enroll into sports school to continue my swimming and to take part in even higher level competitions. However, different path was chosen for me, as it might have been seen as too far away from home and too dangerous for a girl. At this news my confidence and excitement was lost and I felt invisible. In the next few years I got bullied, I felt like no one really understood me, like I didn't quite fit in. Although I didn't have it easy, I appreciated the few friends who cared and loved the authentic me.

I have many wonderful childhood memories filled with meaningful experiences. One I cherished most was nourishing my spirit by attending the *God's Children* meetings at our parish. There, we would gather to read the Bible, reflect on its teachings, engage in deep conversations, and sing songs praising God. It was fun, engaging and aligned on so many levels. Another of my fondest memories was sitting by the large window in my room of our third-floor apartment, sketching the breathtaking views of the sprawling gardens with vibrant sunsets. It was my way of expressing myself and feeling connected to the beauty around me.

My parents are caring and hardworking middle class workers. They expressed their love through verbal discipline, out of a desire for good for their children. Given their limited resources and knowledge, they did the best they could. They did not know any better apart from what they have seen their parents do as parents. My mother is a professional seamstress, and my father, a truck driver who is now retired. They often struggled with financial instability and their own insecurities, which in turn fueled their arguments and often created an intense atmosphere at home.

As a result of many challenges and demands of growing family, my mother displayed remarkable courage when she decided to move to the United States alone to improve our family's financial situation. I chose to follow her footsteps just couple years later as I dearly missed her. I continued my education in New York City. My interest in creative design and technology flourished, as I delved into working on the novelty then, the Macintosh computers, Apple Macs now - a passion that began back in

Poland and continued in the United States. I pursued a degree in Art and Advertising Design at New York City College of Technology, which set the foundation for my career as a graphic designer. My early professional experiences included working for *Cigar Aficionado Magazine and* New York advertising agency where I created artwork for printed media.

Although all was new to me, I settled easily as I was surrounded by fantastic friends, extended family and my dear mom. I felt like I had truly found my place and my people. It gave me a sense of belonging that I had longed for a very long time. Every gathering was filled with laughter, shared stories and a deep sense of connection. Whether it was a casual afternoon spent catching up or a lively celebration of some sort, there was always an atmosphere of acceptance and joy. These relationships were and continue to be super special as we formed a close-knit circle of deep friendships and support.

Our love story...

My husband and I met in a rather serendipitous way. We knew it was destiny, when we found out we both moved to New York City within just two days of each other. Three years from that date, our paths magically crossed when a mutual friend invited us to a party. We were introduced that day and soon decided to meet again for our first official date. Our relationship progressed with every moment we spent together. Six months later we were happily engaged and started to make plans for our life together.

Our love story is filled with incredible adventures, road trips across the country and thrilling roller coaster rides - much like the life ahead of us.

It was love at first sight. Our connection, our bond and our commitment felt extraordinary right from the beginning. That initial glance, the first embrace, our first dance and his first gentle kiss on my décolletage - I knew, without a doubt, we were meant to be together.

We started our life together by having two fabulous weddings. One was an intimate and glorious. It took place in Las Vegas in Little White Chapel, with just the two of us present. The second one was held in the

Big Apple - New York - in a gorgeous polish church in Brooklyn then we continued extravagant and joyous reception in lovely Italian reataurant. We had a splendid and gleeful wedding with all of our family and friends who traveled from other states and from around the world to be there with us. It was our way of creating a loving and connected union. Since then, we were blessed too give life to three kind, ambitious and intelligent children.

In 2005, we moved to the United Kingdom where I worked as Graphic Designer for a fashion lifestyle magazine and then Head of Design for the U.K.'s premier regional magazine. Next, I became Marketing Specialist for a blue-chip global corporate construction company, creating branded publications, printed and digital marketing assets, books for architects, promotional items, sportswear for charity sporting events and product packaging. These jobs allowed me not only to hone in my skills - but an opportunity to work with world-class global brands.

I thought this was my career path for life, I thought I would retire working in corporate company. At that point, I had worked there for nearly seven years, believing it was a secure and stable job for life. Although initialy I was content with what I have acomplished in my career, I still felt the hunger for soul fulfillment and a sense of contribution to society. I felt there was more to my life. Yet, I continued to ignore that inner gut feeling and did nothing about it.

Then, one sunny day during my break I decided to take a walk along a path near lush, green golf course. As I strolled, I found myself asking God for guidance, as one often does in quiet, reflective moments. "How long will you let me continue to be in this state of not truly feeling fulfilled? Is there nothing more to life? What other way have I been called to serve my family, my community and others?" Six months later, I got my answer. On January 7th, just after New Year's celebrations, I was handed redundancy letter. Many employees were made redundant due to restructuring of the marketing deparment.

The experience of being made redundant from a 'secure job' felt like the rug was pulled from underneath my feet, and I hit rock bottom - an emotional bottom like I've never experienced before. This unexpected turn left me devastated and depressed for more than six months - and without any emotional support. My family and close friends extended a supportive hand during that challenging time, for which I am forever grateful. Months later, I came across a book titled *Feel the Fear and Do It Anyway* by Susan Jeffers. It gave me the courage to take back control of my life - and even to start my own business. That was my leap of faith into entrepreneurship.

My journey of personal growth and transformation had begun the day I chose 'Me'.

One day a dear friend - I call her 'My Angel' - saw a potential in me that I had long overlooked and forgotten. I got introduced to a transformational leadership training led by powerful international trainers such as Lisa Kalmin, Lynne Sheridan, Judith Rich, Myrna Gonzalez and Michael Strasner. This experience was truly a life changing pivotal time for me. It was the first time I experienced this level of support from open-hearted, generous, loving souls who genuinely saw me, empowered me and believed in my extended potential.

The transformational leadership training was so much more than just an educational experience; it was a personal metamorphosis. For the first time, I came out from behind the scenes and played full out and embraced both, my grateness as well as my limitations. The trainers, the coaches and other students hugely impacted and inspired me to come out from hiding and start shining with my heart and my soul sharring my gifts generously with others.

At 44, I found my why. It's both super ambitious and extremely fulfilling. I am on a mission to support and empower women to let go of what's not serving them so they can step into their power and courage to create extraordinary results, whether in professional or private life, as it is one. We have one shot at this game called life, why not play full out. This is a perfect time to ask you powerful soul, what do YOU truly want in life? What is YOUR why?

Life is like a roller coaster ride...A few years later, life presented me with new turbulent challenges and therefore a plethora of opportunities compelling me to step up, show up and play even bigger.

These experiences pushed me far beyond my comfort zone, encouraging me to take on greater responsibilities. It became clear that I was being called to grow and expand my impact. This time it was heartbreaking as my child's health declined. This news deeply shook and affected my whole family. The experience was overwhelming and full of uncertainty. Without my leadership skills, tools and distinctions, I would have been paralyzed by helplessness, I would become a victim of fear and worry - unable to take any action forward.

But I didn't. It wasn't about me.

Yes, I felt all of the above and much more, and I was able to not only manage my emotions but also to support my family whilst keeping the vision of my son's health. I was incredibly grateful for the tools and strategies I had gained throughout my leadership journey. There were multiple moving pieces to manage like appointments, tests, sessions, events, household, trainings, clients, friends and family events. And on top of that, I was still pursuing my personal vision and goals. For many women, such a crisis might lead to abandoning personal ambitions to focus solely on family. It might lead to emotional overwhelm or burnout.

However, I know that it is possible to create both. I am the example of that. I learned that I could grow as a person, maintain my professional aspirations, and support my family simultaneously even in such difficult times. If navigating these challenges was possible for me, it's possible for you as well. It's all about your leadership and the right support.

I was confident that recovery was achievable and fully trusted that, in the end, everything would be alright. With the additional support from loved ones, the guidance of experienced coaches, and the grace of God, I felt reassured and uplifted. These combined sources of strength and encouragement helped me navigate through the tough period, trusting all was on the path to recovery and healing.

There was no stopping me; I chose me once again as I embarked on the next level of extraordinary training, the Ph.D. Mastery of Leadership training with Michael Strasner. This next level of leadership involved learning all of the distinctions, embodiing and implementing them everywhere and everyday. We trained to guide, empower and lead teams.

I continued to advance, finally owning and using the power of my voice to influence and enroll others into what's possible for them.

This time, I've experienced transformation firsthand, when I chose to let go of my lifelong fear of public speaking.

I can still remember the horrifying feeling...

When being called to speak in front of the teacher and classmates, I felt like I was on fire, shaking with nervousness. I would experience brain fog, blurred vision, and forget everything I studied. The moment I was asked to answer a question or read aloud, a painful knot would twist and hurt my stomach.

Even a few years ago, I would avoid speaking up during corporate meetings, clenching my jaws so tightly that it hurt. This fear was so intense that speaking in front of even a small group of people was extremely stressful, let alone addressing a large audience.

One encouraging moment happened when despite my extreme nerves the passion for this project allowed me to speak during a large team meeting sharring my team's achievement. We just completed designing a line of branded merchandise, and decided that all proceeds from the sales would go to a charity dedicated rescueing and caring for children who were rescued from trafficking. This victory was a great start, showcasing how I could actually overcome my fear of speaking in public, only with persistence, passion and courage.

The next leap was the moment I never thought was possible for me, up until then. I got invited to speak on stage in Paris on International Women's Day Conference in early 2024. My wonderful 20-year-old daughter accompanied me there and was my biggest supporter. She witnessed her mother - who once struggled to say "hello" to the camera - now on inernational stage addressing and engaging a large audience present in the room and on global livestream.

I danced onto the stage to one of Shakira's songs, as she greatly inspires me. I spoke about secrets of thriving with passion in life.

It was a 25-minute speech about self-discovery we were never taught at school. 25 minutes! Can you believe it?! Once 5 minutes seemed forever and challenging. I spoke about how to acquire leadership skills to create powerful relationships; authentic living; how to break free from societal expectations and how to take purposeful action to create a vision for life.

This experience was not only a professional milestone, but also a personal goal, demonstrating the power of perseverance, love and self-belief.

The triumph, the cherry on cake and manifestation of my work up until now, led to yours truly hosting a powerful 2.5-hour transformational leadership workshop called *Thrive with Passion, Secrets to Infuse Passion into Every Aspect of Your Life*. My voice has created a powerful impact in 70 people's lives that day - including my friends, family, clients and students. When I was complete, I cried tears of joy, love and pride as I hugged my children and husband.

This newfound confidence in speaking opened a jar of incredible opportunities. It wasn't an overnight change, but a gradual process of chipping away what was not serving me. Through coaching, continuous practice and being willing to feel very uncomfortable, I truly discovered the power of my voice.

A key factor in my jouney of transformation has been the support of others. From my husband's support to the dear friend who introduced me to my first leadership training, to my blessed buddies in this work, and the community of coaches and mentors I've worked with. Having a supportive network has made a significant difference in my journey.

In 2021, I began my path towards fulfilling a long-held vision of launching my own digital magazine. COURAGE Magazine Global, a platform dedicated to empowering women to embrace their authentic selves and to share their stories. The magazine serves as a beacon of inspiration, showcasing tales of courage and strength to support those who are few steps away and need to hear those courageous stories to keep going. In addition, women have the opportunity to advertise their businesses to wider global audience. It aims to support female founders on their journey of growth through shared experiences, networking and sharing their skills and services. We also broadcast interviews with powerful and inspiring women in the community sparking conversations, coaching and valuable insight about business, branding, marketing, health, leadership and relationships with teens and young adults.

As a child, I would daydream about being a TV presenter, envisioning myself interviewing people. As an adult, I have forgotten about this dream, until I chose me. I love hearing success stories about the power of resilience and courage which were created by being inspired by our community. Seeing women step into their power choosing themselves and make meaningful contributions to society which reinforces my belief in the transformative power of love, courage and passion.

My journey is one of continuous growth and dedication to empowering women, whether through my magazine, coaching or personal interactions. My mission is to support women in seeing their fascinating potential that is yet to be discovered. I am committed to creating a lasting legacy of transformation, the one that will inspire and uplift women and their families for generations to come.

Through a blend of comprehensive branding strategies, marketing expertise and leadership guidance, I help women like you articulate their unique values, strengths and visions. From creation to crafting compelling narratives that showcase your passion. My aim is to empower you to build a strong, authentic presence that truly resonates with your audience. As I look to the future, I am filled with joy and determination to transform one million lives through leadership training, coaching, visibility and PR. I want to continue creating spaces where others can step into their power, embrace their authentic selves, and achieve their dreams.

There have been significant milestones and events that have shaped who I am today. I now see how every experience, challenge, I was faced with, from lack of confidence, fear of using my voice, to the unexpected job loss and child's illness, all of the m have contributed to my growth. They all taught me adaptability, resilience and power. Each step of the way, I learned valuable lessons that prepared me for the next one.

What is your why, your purpose and passion to making a positive difference in the world?

ABOUT EDITH WOLEK

Edith Wolek

Edith Wolek, CEO and Founder of Emperors Media, Brand Leadership Coaching & Creative Services and publisher of COURAGE Magazine Global, is dedicated to providing support and visibility to women in business through the inspirational magazine and creative marketing assets attracting your prospective clients. With 24 years of experience, Emperors Media offers services in advertising, marketing and branding for SME businesses. Edith's expertise helps entrepreneurs achieve their marketing goals to grow and scale their businesses. Her extended portfolio includes work with blue-chip companies such as Saint-Gobain, Artex, Isover, INCA and design of marketing campaigns for Lexus, Toyota, smart, Mercedes-Benz and more. Edith's achievements include Portfolio Award, Marketing Project Award and Cultivating Customer Intimacy Award.

Edith is a passionate Transformational Leadership Coach, Global Game Changer - Master Leader and International Inspirational Speaker. She is committed to supporting and empowering female entrepreneurs, mothers, CEOs, founders and directors to create a humanity-centred brands. Edith is a proud mother of three intelligent and ambitious children. She and her husband are joyfully celebrating their 25th wedding anniversary, reflecting on a quarter-century of love, unity and commitment.

Website: www.couragemagazineglobal.com
Website: www.edithwolek.com
FB Group: https://www.facebook.com/groups/768612380503843/
Facebook: https://www.facebook.com/edith.emperorsmedia
LinkedIn: https://www.linkedin.com/in/edithwolek
Instagram: https://www.instagram.com/edith_emperorsmedia/
Email: Edith@emperorsmedia.com

FROM ENABLER, TO ENLISTED, TO ENTREPRENEUR

"Mrs. Young, this is detective Parker with the St. George Police Department. We have arrested your husband on charges of possession with intent to distribute."

It was a Friday like any other. Mildly warm and sunny, not unusual for February in southern Utah. The clock ticked to 4 p.m. and I was content knowing that I had only an hour or so of work left before the three-day weekend.

Working in a busy real estate office at a time when the housing market was in all sorts of disarray, I would've expected it to be busier, but I was happy that this particular Friday had been quiet. Until I received that call from the police department.

"We have also impounded your vehicle. If there are any personal items you need out of it, you will need to come to the impound yard to get them."

The call continued for a few minutes, but I wasn't really listening. I remember answering a few questions with stunned "I don't know's" - and then wondering how I was going to travel the 25 miles home with no car.

It was around 4:20 p.m. when the phone call ended. Even though it was Friday afternoon, there were a few people in the office. I got up and quietly closed and locked my office door before completely breaking down. I didn't want anyone coming in and seeing me completely broken down. Only 2 people knew that I was married to an addict and quietly dealing with the struggle of being his star enabler. I was not in a position to answer any questions or give an explanation to any well-meaning colleagues looking to console me.

Maybe it was the events of the last 20 minutes, or maybe it was the pregnancy hormones kicking into high gear, but I felt so nauseous I couldn't stand up or even open my eyes. You see, a mere 17 days earlier we had found out we were going to be parents. So there I was, at roughly 10 weeks pregnant, wondering not only how to get home for the night, but if I would soon become a single parent.

I managed to compose myself and just before 5 p.m., I called Enterprise for a rental car, because they'll pick you up - and I really needed a "pick me up" at that moment. Problem #1 solved.

I managed to pull myself together and mostly stop crying over the next 25 minutes. The lady from Enterprise picked me up and luckily she wasn't big on making conversation because I was in no shape for small talk.

With impeccable timing, my boss called while I was at Enterprise.

You might think that would have been an awkward conversation… "Oh hey boss, I'm getting a rental car because my husband and my car have just been arrested…"

But that wasn't the case at all. In fact, my boss and his wife, who are like family to me now, were the two people at work who knew what I was going through. They had been dealing with an addict in their family as well and we had been able to support each other over the prior eight to nine months while we all navigated the struggles of loving an addict and trying to help them while not acting as the devout enablers that would only make their habits harder to break. (None of us were very good at avoiding the title of enabler.)

I was at the rental counter when he called. I simply answered with "Hey, can I call you back in about a half hour, Karl has been arrested and my car is at the impound lot." He simply said "Of course" and we hung up.

I finally secured a rental car and found my way to the Impound lot to collect my personal belongings from the car. We were in the middle of moving because we had just lost our home in bankruptcy, and the trunk was loaded with boxes.

I moved my things into the rental car and had a brief conversation with the detective. Then I went home.

During the evening, I would have more conversations with the arresting detective and other investigators. They asked if I would meet them at my house (the one we were moving out of), to which I agreed, to let them in to search for whatever they thought was there. They thought they were going to find a drug lab, but did not. I had absolutely nothing to hide and I knew they weren't going to find what they thought was there.

I also had a conversation with my mom in which she said flat out that I should divorce the love of my life. I stopped her right there and said this is my choice, not yours. That was the end of that.

When all was said and done, and I finally returned to the home we had just moved into, I was exhausted. But also relieved.

I slept better that night than I had in years. It was like the weight of worrying that had been holding me down for so long was suddenly lifted.

After several years of not knowing if my life partner was going to turn up dead or maybe not turn up at all, I knew that things were finally going to change. I didn't know how, but from that pivotal moment, our life together would never be the same.

I drifted off to sleep around 11 p.m. and I slept until 8:00 the next morning. As much as I might have wanted it to be, I knew it hadn't been a bad dream and that I was now in a very real situation where attorneys would be involved, I might end up raising my first child alone, and the only relationship with my husband would be through a telephone and tv screen.

But the sun shone a little bit brighter that day. I knew in my heart that all would be ok. Even though all the walls were crashing down around me, it almost felt like I was floating above it all, tethered only by my love for my husband and my stubbornness to not let some damn drug ruin my marriage.

His arrest was one of those checkpoints in life, a sort of point of no return. No matter what happened next, for me, there was no going back to the old life. Over the next two months there would be visits to the jail, court appearances, and federal drug charges levied against my husband. That last one turned out to be the biggest blessing and best possible outcome in this situation.

When charged federally, he was assigned an attorney at no cost to us (due to the impending bankruptcy). That attorney wasted no time working on getting him released from county lockup so that he could be with me during my pregnancy and while we waited for the first federal court date.

He was able to spend the next 18 months at home, becoming a father, working hard on his sobriety and recovery, and learning how to live free of the chains that addiction brings. I too had to learn to live in this new and very welcomed "normal".

After spending several years compartmentalizing my emotions, hyperfocusing on work, binge-watching TV shows to escape the reality of the situation, and putting on a show that everything was great, it was very refreshing to simply be and live in a natural state of happiness and gratitude without needing those things to keep my mind busy.

Imagine being trapped in quicksand for over three years, struggling just to keep your head up and slowly fading away as the weight of the sand overtakes you...wanting so desperately to escape and run away from it, but being completely consumed by it. That is how it feels to love an addict, enable an addict, and attempt to make a normal life with an addict. But in the instant that it all changed, when we escaped the hold of the quicksand, we were able to run faster than we ever imagined and love harder than we thought possible.

We lived the next 18 months in as much happiness as possible. Our son was born, and we worked hard to recover from our bankruptcy while attending regular court dates and waiting for sentencing to happen.

Finally on February 6, 2009, we went to Federal court in Salt Lake City, Utah. Even with glowing recommendations from the probation team and statements from family members, the judge sentenced my husband to 54 months in prison at a federal facility in California. While this was a lot less than the maximum allowed sentence of 10 years, at that moment, it felt like 54 months was an eternity.

With 6 weeks to self-surrender, we made sure to spend every moment together as a family making memories and preparing for what was to come. Never did I imagine myself preparing to become a single mom to an 18-month-old, but there we were.

On March 20, 2009, we delivered my husband to the federal prison outside of Taft, California and then made the trip back to southern Utah to begin the next chapter of life.

Over the course of the next three years, I would experience a wide range of emotions - from depression to anxiety, self-doubt, and more. Adjusting to life as a single parent was not easy, so I took it a day at a time. I reconnected with my passion for music and went back to college to finish my bachelor's degree in music performance. As if single parenting and working full time wasn't already consuming all my time.

Just as I had during my husband's addiction, I found every external focus I could to keep me busy and focused on anything except the reality of the situation. Luckily, I had my son there to keep me grounded. He will never know just how much he saved me during those years.

Life continued, my son grew, and I bought a house for us to call home. I was successful at work, made the trip to California to see my husband a few times a year, and learned that I was much stronger than I ever gave myself credit for. Then came another pivotal conversation, this time with my private music instructor at the university.

"The Marines are looking for clarinet players and they want you to audition. Are you interested?"

I'm not usually one to be speechless, but I was. Silence hung in the room. It was as if the walls were holding their breath, waiting for me to say something.

As the walls turned blue in the face, I finally spoke, and they could catch their breath. I decided that it wouldn't hurt to at least meet with the recruiters and see what they had to say. This wasn't a commitment, I could say "no, thank you" and carry on with my life. But maybe, just maybe, a little part of me was saying "do this, you will never get the chance again."

I come from a deep legacy of military service and was intrigued by the opportunity. Both my parents, two uncles, numerous other relatives, and my father-in-law have all served our country. But I had a son and a job, a house, and responsibilities. I couldn't just rush into something new. Or could I? I figured there was no harm in at least meeting with the recruiters to see what they had to say.

I decided to take the meeting, but I didn't tell anyone. The only person that knew about this meeting was my instructor, because I wanted to go into it with an open, unbiased mind. Besides, my parents served in the

Air Force, and I couldn't let them know I was about to show them up by joining the Marines…at nearly 29 years old.

Was I crazy? Who joins the military at 29?

When I met with the recruiter, I made sure he was aware of the situation with my husband and that I had a son. I made it abundantly clear that if I decided to move forward, I would not be able to go anywhere until after my husband was released from prison and was settled at home.

Because of the demand for musicians and the difficulty of finding qualified individuals to enlist, the recruiter was willing to work with me on whatever I needed. I still wasn't immediately sold, but I did feel a little spark of excitement as I left the meeting.

Driving home, I got a little lost in my thoughts…What if I do this? What if I don't do this? If I don't, I would have to live with the fact that when I had the chance to serve my country, in a special way, I declined. When I had the opportunity to do something great, I passed it up. That was not going to happen.

I was still on the fence, and I stayed there for a few weeks. It was the holidays, and I didn't want to rush into any big decisions while also juggling the stress of Christmas travel and get-togethers.

After 2011 faded to memory and 2012 came front and center, the recruiter called me to check in and offered me a meeting with his commanding officer. He knew I was teetering between making the commitment and telling him to take a hike. I took up the offer to meet with the Commanding Officer and a time was arranged that worked with my schedule.

I let the Commanding Officer know about my current situation, the order of events that would need to take place before I could commit, and that I would need flexibility with the training schedule due to being a full-time employee, full time student, and full-time parent. If they would agree to all that I needed, I would commit to doing what I needed to do to be ready to go when the time came.

I told them I could not leave for boot camp until my husband was home and settled which was roughly eight months away at this point and they agreed to make sure I would not be required to leave prior to that. I felt good about the prospect of enlisting in the military. I took some more time to think about it and I finally told my parents. My dad was ecstatic, my mom not so much, but she understood the need to pursue the opportunity and she supported my decision.

I also had to tell my husband. But I couldn't just call him up at the prison. I had to wait for him to call me one night because it was a one-way phone line. When he called, I said the words no man ever wants to hear: "We need to talk."

Silence.

More silence.

(Me now wondering if my husband has passed out or is just holding his breath in fear of what is next.)

Finally, I heard him breathe so I said, "I want to join the Marines as a musician."

More silence.

Me wondering again if he has passed out from the surprise. Finally, "You want to do what?"

"I've been approached by a recruiter and offered the chance to audition for placement as a musician in the Marines and I want to do it."

My husband later told me that he knew for certain I was going to ask for a divorce on that phone call. As soon as I said we needed to talk, he mentally prepared himself for that. Instead, the joke was on him! He was stuck with me and when he got home from his extended stay at "summer camp" (that's what we called the prison!), I was going to leave, and he would get to be a single parent for a while.

I had my work cut out for me to enlist, not musically but physically. I had to shave 2 1/2 minutes off my 1 1/2-mile run-time, learn how to do 60 crunches in 2 minutes and work on my pull-ups. I also had to take the ASVAB, which is like a watered-down miniature version of those standardized tests they make you take in 11th grade.

Remember I'm nearly 29 at this point and I haven't taken a math class since I was 17 - but the minimum required score for enlisting in the music program is 50 so I figured I'd be OK. I also had a performance audition over the phone to make sure I could actually play before they had the audition coordinator travel all the way to Utah to hear me in person. February 1, 2012 was testing day. I went to the recruiter's office and met up with him and about four other potential recruits that would also be taking the test. They ranged in age from 17 to 19 and were completely panicked about this test.

We piled into the govvy (slang term for government vehicle) and headed to the National Guard station where the test was administered. I gave the soldier my ID and dealt with the "How *OLD* are you?" nonsense that would be the norm for the entirety of my military career and I got assigned to a computer.

I was the first one done with the test - I got it done with about 30 minutes to spare. I notified the moderator that I was done, and to my surprise all the youngsters were still working on it, so I sat, and I waited. (Remember we all rode together so I couldn't just get in the car and leave.) They don't give you your score until everyone is done so I didn't even know how I did.

Finally, everyone was done, and the recruiter came back to get us. The soldier at the front handed each of us a ripped off corner of notebook paper with a number on it: our test score. Mine was 98. I had been out of high school for 11 years at this point and I got a 98 on the ASVAB! The recruiter was floored, and everyone else was speechless, all scoring in the 60s or 70s. So now I was famous for being old and smart!

Two days later, after a full day of work and two university band performances, I had my in-person audition to qualify for the musician enlistment program. For the audition, they have you play some technical items, a portion of a prepared piece and then sight-read two marches. Sight-reading is basically when they pick a random march from a giant binder, give you 2 minutes to look it over, and then say "Go!" and you play it.

I was understandably tired at this point, but I felt good about my audition. The scoring system was from one to four - kind of like a GPA in school. Two was the minimum eligible score, and four was perfect. A score of three allowed you to choose your duty station prior to enlistment. I took a deep breath and got my score: 3.0. "Congratulations - you get to pick your duty station."

I was very proud of myself, but this was the easy part. The next six months of getting my body into shape to meet the physical requirements of the Marine Corps would prove to be one of the most challenging, yet most rewarding, periods of my adult life.

After my audition, life went back to normal for a while. Each day, I went from work to school to parenting to physical training. I had weekly check-ins with my recruiters, weigh-ins to make sure I was where I was supposed to be, and evaluations that ensured I was getting faster and stronger.

I turned 29 in March that year and had to get a waiver before I could officially enlist in the Marine Corps - because 28 is the cutoff. But at least I didn't have to get a permission slip from my mom because I was too young!

On April 13th, 2012, I enlisted into the delayed entry program with the scheduled date for boot camp of August 27th. Now it was real, this was happening. I continued to work hard to get in shape, maintain my musical prowess, watch my son grow and learn, and then finally got to bring my husband home from prison in late July. That was a wonderful day filled with emotion and excitement. We were complete.

Over the coming weeks, we all prepared ourselves for me to leave at the end of August. My husband transitioned into dad mode very easily. Just as I was preparing to leave, I got a phone call from the recruiting station.

They had an opportunity for me to wait six more weeks to leave and get a sign-on bonus. They wanted to pay me $6000 to wait six weeks to leave. I thought, "OK -no problem!" That was a no-brainer - and of course, I accepted.

At last, the big day had come. In early October of 2012, it was my turn to go to boot camp. We said our temporary goodbyes, knowing that the next time we would talk would be 12 weeks later. I was sad for a bit, but I knew I was doing the right thing and that we would all be stronger for it. The next day was go-time - one final weigh-in and a drug test later and I was off to the airport, bound for South Carolina.

Finally, all the work I had done to get my body and mind to the required standards, while keeping my musicianship up and mentally preparing myself was about to pay off. (I won't go into the details of boot camp - I could write an entire book on that alone!) Just know that I pushed myself harder mentally and physically than I had ever done. I did things I never dreamed I would have been able to do before. All the trials life had put me through to this point gave me the strength and mental toughness needed to succeed and excel in boot camp, combat training, and follow-on school.

I realized that my path had been taking me in the direction I needed to go to be ready for the opportunities that lay ahead. Had I not gone through what I went through with my husband, I would not have had the mental fortitude needed to leave my family and serve in the military.

Although my military career was cut short by an injury (and I still suffer with chronic pain as a result), I would not change my decision to enlist. I can proudly tell my children that when I was given the opportunity to serve my country in a way that so very few can, I accepted that challenge. I had the strength to move forward when all odds were against me.

I separated from the military in October 2015 and returned to Utah to finally be reunited with my family.

They had remained in Utah throughout my enlistment. We saw each other on long weekends, leave periods, and when my son would come live with me during the summer between school years. Transitioning back to civilian life was a challenge for me, but it was so nice to be with my family again. I went back to performing with the local symphony. We had our second child, I went back to work, and finally, in 2017, I finished my bachelor's degree after 16 years of on-again, off-again college.

Now you'd think we'd been through a lot at this point, but about a year later I got the bright idea to apply for graduate school. What can I say? I'm a glutton for punishment! I did have a purpose though. Over the prior 10 years of working in real estate, attending college, performing, and serving in the military, I noticed one painfully obvious truth: many people struggle to communicate effectively, and it affects their lives both personally and professionally. I had the idea that I could use my experience, my expertise, my story, and a little more education to help others hone their skills as communicators. We are all capable of communicating at a higher level, but too often we leave those skills by the wayside.

I got to work and dove into my master's program head first. Once again my strength would be tested, but I knew I could handle it. How? Because I had already pushed myself to what I thought was my limit. And every time I thought I was there, my limits simply moved farther away. I broke my own ceilings every time I pushed for something new. And that leads me to my point: life has taught me that the things we go through give us the mental strength to go through what comes next. That strength then influences our decisions and goals.

There's a saying that "the only limits we face are the ones we place on ourselves." I believe this to be true. Mental toughness is a muscle. It has to be exercised, stretched, and challenged to grow. When we are in the thick of it, it can seem impossible to keep going. But just like in bodybuilding, when muscles fatigue, they need rest to rebuild. Then they get stronger. The strength comes from reaching the limit then pushing it forward over and over again.

After separating from the military, I found myself back to work in the real estate industry because I had worked there before - it was familiar. This time I was working on the mortgage side of things, so it was something new but still in the realm of my prior experience. I was pregnant with my daughter and needed the additional income, so I had to get a job. I knew that I could work in the industry because I already had connections there, I wouldn't have to fight to be hired, and I wouldn't have to search very long to find a good-paying job. I didn't mind the work, but it was something I fell into out of necessity rather than from choice. I met some great friends along the way and learned a lot, but I also worked with some people that weren't the best fit for me. I stayed with it out of need.

One day I looked at my husband and I said, "You know what? I want us to move to Oregon. Let's pack up the house and sell everything - we're leaving." And we did just that. We packed up, sold or gave away nearly everything we had, and we moved to Oregon.

This one choice allowed me to reinvent myself.

I was able to connect with new people, make new friends, and really explore the dreams that I had. Through the people I met, I learned that I could design my own life. I didn't have to stay with what was familiar simply because it was comfortable. I could choose to do something new. I could choose to be fulfilled. I could choose to dare greatly, to be brave and to take courageous action. It took me a little while to really believe them, but eventually I decided to take my chance. In early 2024 I gave myself permission to leave my job in the mortgage field to pursue my dream of owning my own business as a speaking and speechwriting coach, after running it as a side hustle for a few months.

While my business is still relatively new, I am truly enjoying all the things I am learning, all the connections I'm making, and the people that I am helping through the services I provide. I love being a speaking coach, leadership communication expert, speechwriting consultant, and performance trainer. I truly believe that all of the experiences I've gone through - as well as the strength, mental toughness, and fortitude I have gained - have helped me get to this point. Without all those trials, I don't think I would have been brave enough to take the leap to not only move to a completely different state where I knew only two people, but also to leave my job and its secure paycheck for the great unknown. That is what you commit to when you own your own business.

If you're reading this and living a life that pays the bills but leaves you feeling unfulfilled, take stock. If you feel like you're not living up to your potential, or that you have reached your own limits, I encourage you to think about what you really want, and then lean on your community to help you create it. Learn from those around you, look back on your life experiences, and look at just how strong, courageous, and smart you are. Don't be afraid to live your life on your own terms. And if owning a business is part of those terms, I am here cheering you on.

ABOUT APRIL YOUNG

April Young

April Young is the founder of Stage Savvy Speakers, where she coaches aspiring and novice speakers to build their skills and confidence as they prepare to take the stage. With a rich background as a United States Marine, lifelong musician and a Masters degree in communication, she brings a harmonious blend of musical insight and communication expertise to her coaching practice.

April empowers women to take center-stage as speakers and presenters for all audiences. She specializes in helping women who are held back by self-doubt, anxiety, and stage fright. Utilizing a unique blend of coaching strategies, musical performance principles, and hard-learned life lessons, April helps her clients build unshakeable confidence, a captivating story-based message, and powerful stage presence.

Whether you're an aspiring speaker or already in a role that requires public speaking, April offers the tailored guidance you need to confidently craft and deliver impactful presentations to any audience.

Website: www.stagesavvyspeakers.com
Facebook: https://www.facebook.com/stagesavvyspeakers
LinkedIn: https://www.linkedin.com/company/stagesavvyspeakers
Instagram: www.instagram.com/stagesavvyspeakers

Jamie Young

THE $300 GAMBLE: FROM CORPORATE BURNOUT TO BUILDING A SUCCESSFUL BUSINESS

I was 12 years old. My mom and I stood at the checkout with a cart full of groceries, and my mom's check bounced - again. Standing there, I felt deep humiliation at her being unable to buy the most basic of life's needs - food.

That was the first time I experienced true embarrassment - a deep feeling of insecurity and scarcity.

In the following years, I knew I wanted to create a different life. I desperately desired safety and security for my adult life. From an early age, the message of the world was clear to me: I would not be given an easy life and would have to forge my own path to security.

I planned to work hard and climb the corporate ladder - and boy, did I do that! I started my working life in the hospitality industry first as a waitress, where I worked hard and made excellent money. Then, I was promoted to my first management job at 20, and I didn't stop there. I worked long hours as an assistant general manager, sometimes seven days a week. I began to feel the stress, anxiety, and pressure of climbing the corporate ladder, realizing that my salary broke down to an hourly wage that had me practically working for free. I was never free of my job. Even on my days off, my phone rang with someone on the other end needing me to solve some problem. I was on my path to security, but at what cost?

When I was 27, I was offered my dream position as a hotel general manager. In the middle of the call, I realized I was done. My current position as assistant general manager had led to my being in complete burnout - so I gave my 30-day notice on the spot. I was shocked that I did that, but I was not upset. After my last day as an assistant GM, I went home and changed the ringer on my phone because every time it rang, I could still feel the triggering anxiety. It only confirmed that my decision was the right one.

When I left that dream job, I was up for anything. That left me open to enter a new, scary territory: sales. As it turns out, I'm pretty good at it.

A family friend was in sales, and he was working a job that sold online ads. I said yes to trying cold-call sales. I focused on selling online ads to Canadian realtors and made more money than I did in any of my hospitality jobs. The financial crisis was beginning to hit the real estate market, and those who wanted to win knew that marketing was the way to stay in business. The beauty of this job was that I could go home when I hit my goal. Some days, I met my goal early and left by noon!

This sales job opened my eyes to a way of working that was completely different from what I had experienced before. I showed up in an honest and authentic way and listened to my clients' needs. When the product didn't fit their needs, I simply thanked them for their time and told them this was not the product for them. I learned I could make money, serve my clients, and still have freedom.

Getting introduced to a commission-based sales environment (heading into the 2008 financial crisis, no less) showed me that being brave and showing up to the plate with a plan and a strategy was the secret to success. I spent most evenings and early mornings reading books on sales and the buyers' mindset, drilling down on becoming better at my craft. My favorites to this day are: *Good to Great* by Jim Collins, anything from John Maxwell, and old school Dale Carnegie's *How to Win Friends & Influence People*.

However, three years in, the realtor online ad sales became saturated, and I started looking for another sales job. I was hired by the Portland Women's Expo and started running a sales team responsible for bringing in sponsors and vendors. I loved it. I was very successful at renewing vendors at the Women's Expo for the next show because I listened to their needs.

Really early on, I saw that the people who renewed were successful because they set and measured a tangible goal for success at the show, often leveraging promotional products to get emails from potential clients. I started using the stories of successful expo vendors to inspire others to think differently about their tangible goals and how to leverage their branded promotional materials. It is a skillset I use with my clients today.

In January 2018 I was invited to a promotional products distributor trade show while I was working at the Women's Expo show. At this tradeshow, I immediately knew I had to start selling promotional products like pens, lip balms, banners, tablecloths, and swag because all my expo vendors were already buying these items from internet sources.

Entrepreneurship was not my plan. Growing up poor, all I wanted and valued was safety, security, and guaranteed comfort.

But I couldn't let the idea go.

Exactly one month after the trade show, I devised a business plan and officially structured my business, Attagirl Promotions LLC, which I still work under today. I met with a CPA who helped me file for an LLC and a business license. She asked me what my personal contribution was, and I replied, "I have $300." Two hundred and seventy-five dollars was the cost of my business licenses.

With my business set up legally, I then needed to find customers. With a full-time job, family, and an eight-month-old baby at home, I committed to three networking events per week. That turned out to be the recipe for my launching success. It was exhausting, but it worked. I wouldn't leave an event until I met three new business contacts with cards, and then I would immediately reach out and email those businesses. The added bonus was that some of my best friendships came from networking.

At the one-year mark of my business, I quit my full-time job with the Expo to run my promotional products company full-time. My success did not come just from selling products. I saw early on the incredible opportunity that branded apparel and merchandise had to offer a business - but I could see that deciding what branded materials to invest in was the most overwhelming decision for a business owner to make.

Recognizing the overwhelm from my clients early on, I decided to take the driver's seat and offer a simple process to ensure a perfect match. I listened to what they wanted, and made recommendations on products, decoration style, and products that reflect their brand's image. My superpower is to really help my business clients find the best marketing tools for them to increase visibility and stickiness. By helping create strategies and plans based on my client's goals, I quickly became known as "Jamie Young, the Swagologist."

Fast-forward to 2020, when the Pandemic hit us. That summer, my phone rang off the hook for screen-printed T-shirts. I had never sold so many event T-shirts! That led me to start looking for equipment to print my own shirts and bring the system in-house. I'm pretty sure my husband thought I was crazy. I told him I would teach myself through YouTube videos (an epic fail that led to a lot of tears - but no printed shirts).

Through a friend, I found a local couple that had just retired their screen printing business but still had their equipment and client list. I paid them to teach me to screen print and bought their commercial equipment and client list.

Buying their client list was a valuable lesson learned. Looking back, I wish I would have asked more questions and vetted the list for the type of clients on the list, as well as their reorder potential. The majority of their list turned out to be team sports, and during the Pandemic, that was one thing that was not happening. Half of the clients on the list weren't in business anymore. The screen printing business that provided the list had been shut for three or four months, so many of their clients had already found other screen printers.

So, I fell back on the tools from my previous job and started cold-calling businesses.

I have always been haunted by the words "scarcity," "fear," and "poverty." And as a result, I often have the misguided notion that I can work my way out of any problem. Yet what I discovered is that when you serve a need, people will love your approach. In reality, I don't sell a product - not even one that solves a problem or reaches a goal. What I do is fulfill a need and provide a marketing plan with a strategy session for my clients to reach their goals. When my clients win, my business wins.

Screen Printing was the next iteration of my business, and I rebranded it as Uptown Screen Printing. In the early days, we could barely fill the 1,000 sq ft space we leased in the Battle Ground Plaza. We furnished the shop with donated shelves and display cabinets and pieced together a working showroom. By mid-2024, we had outgrown our space and expanded into a larger one.

Growing pains were difficult, but having an experienced business community to rely on was invaluable. We have been through all the stages of growth. We served 227 clients in 2020 and 740 clients in 2023. We increased our business 105% in 2021 from the previous year, 167% in 2022 from 2021 and an additional 33% in 2023 from 2022.

One of the recipes for success I have always leaned into was coaching. I have always had a coach. When I was doing sales, I had a speaking and sales coach. I now have a leadership coach to help me lead my employees. It has always been helpful to have people to lean on when needing advice. When I was struggling early on to know when to hire an employee, I asked for wise counsel from other business leaders. And the advice they gave me was right. Our business doubled every time we hired a new employee.

At the end of the day, you just can't do everything alone. Early on, I buried myself in information from people who had already done it. Community is power. Try things. Diversify. I know my buckets, and know my lane. You can't be an expert in everything. I pay the bookkeeper because I spent more time doing my books wrong and having someone fix them than getting them done right the first time. Lean on the expert and stay in your own lane.

I also let my family hold me accountable so I am not chained to my business. There are times I get up early to work before my family wakes up, but I definitely respect my family enough to squeeze work into 9 to 5 so I have plenty of time for them. I love the freedom to be able to work remotely and define my own day.

If I could go back and tell myself one thing at the beginning of my entrepreneurial journey, it would be to trust the process and know that I am right where I am supposed to be. I am on my journey, not someone else's. It is easy to look at someone else and think that is where I need to be. But my journey is different. My goals are different from those of other business owners.

I have built a really great business, but I am not done yet. When one of my clients in Oregon was running for Miss Oregon, I was impressed by how she leveraged the pageant to bring more awareness to her platform for small businesses against sex trafficking. That got me thinking about myself, my business, and what really mattered to me. In early 2024, I applied to the Washington America Pageants to run for Mrs. Washington America to build more awareness around what made my heart beat - my community and small businesses.

Helping women in business is one of my passion projects. And I really have a heart for the underdog. I want to use my platform to bring attention to women in business in my community who show up and are willing to put in the work. I am not the typical pageant girl. I want to celebrate and uplift women who have struggled through the tears to make things happen.

Next, I ran for Mrs. Washington. What an eye-opening experience! I was very nervous about entering pageants. But I found that not only did my community really show up for me the last three years, but they were also willing to join in on this new adventure through sponsorships. I went to pageant boot camp with Washington America Pageants and was greeted with hugs, carbs, wine, and real women. It was an amazing opportunity to build lasting friendships and share my community with a larger audience.

I am no longer driven by the fears and shame of that 12-year-old-girl that stood in that grocery store, humiliated and insecure. Now, as I build my business and take on new challenges, I am motivated by my daughter. Others are watching: other women, employees, and especially my daughter, Olivia.

I have spent years hustling and manifesting grit when I didn't want to show up. I want to quietly inspire my daughter and other women to do the brave thing, love themselves where they are, have faith in themselves, wipe their tears, and get back out there after a setback. I have been inspired by so many women who don't know they have inspired me. I celebrate all the women who showed up for me, living by example. I live what I preach by doing the brave thing; by doing that, I hope to leave a strong legacy for my daughter.

ABOUT JAMIE YOUNG

Jamie Young

Jamie Young, the Swagologist, is passionate about women in business, and she is on a mission to help local businesses succeed with the right branding and swag that helps her clients reach their goals. Truth is, she never wanted to be an entrepreneur. She wanted guaranteed security and a safe job. But on the way to the top of the corporate ladder, Jamie found herself at a crossroads that led down the unexpected path of entrepreneurship.

Armed with a business plan, $300 and a business license, Jamie started looking for customers. Right from the start she worked to ease her client's marketing decision overwhelm and helped them build brand visibility and stickiness with the right marketing tools. Today her company is one of the fastest growing in Clark County, Washington. She has learned how to balance life between her business and family knowing that she's on her own business journey, not someone else's. All she needs to do is keep showing up.

Website: https://www.uptownscreenprinting.com/
Facebook: https://www.facebook.com/UptownScreenPrintingandGifts
LinkedIn: https://www.linkedin.com/in/jamie-young-aa6aa230
Instagram: https://www.instagram.com/uptown_screenprinting/

Made in United States
Troutdale, OR
10/24/2024

23865744R00106